New Ways with Crochet

New Ways with Crochet

Dorothy Standing

Mills & Boon Limited, London

First published in Great Britain 1971 by
Mills & Boon Limited, 17–19 Foley Street, London WIA IDR

© Dorothy Standing 1971

ISBN 0 263.51602.4

Set in Photon Times 11 on 12 pt. by
Richard Clay (The Chaucer Press), Ltd., Bungay, Suffolk
and printed in Great Britain by ·
Fletcher & Son, Ltd., Norwich, Norfolk

Contents

Abbreviations

ch	chain
ss	slip stitch
dc	double crochet
htr	half treble
tr	treble
dtr	double treble
ttr	triple treble
st	stitch
inc	increase
dec	decrease
rep	repeat
sp	space
ch sp	chain space
gr	group
woh	wool over hook
f ch	foundation chain
t ch	turning chain

New International Crochet Hook Numbers are given in addition to the present range, e.g. No 6 (5·00-mm) hook.

About this book

Some women have a guilty feeling if their hands ever lie idle in their laps. For many, crochet has fulfilled this need to be occupied and has been a pleasant and productive occupation, quite inoffensive though often unimaginative. Left a legacy of learning by great-aunts and grandmothers, they crochet extremely well. They've done yards of it, neatly and beautifully, watched scornfully in the past by more fashionable friends.

Now the tables have turned. Those trendy friends want to crochet. There are phone calls, invitations—come to coffee—come to lunch— and DO bring your crochet hook—it's quite easy, isn't it?

Sometimes, then, a curious fact emerges. The able ones, so good at doing it, cannot always read a pattern, cannot name the stitches or decipher the abbreviations. Teaching crochet is beyond them.

And some women cannot crochet at all. For so long has the craft been neglected that it is a closed book to at least two generations and both young and old are crowding to classes, wanting to learn this 'new' art!

This book will help. It will tell those who can't crochet how to do it, and those who can, what to do with it: how to adapt it to modern use, how to treat crochet as a fabric, making it to fit paper patterns of their own or someone else's design, how to use their imagination to produce individual and fashionable clothes and objects which are interesting and original.

A technical chapter explains many of the problems, not always dealt with, which have arisen and been solved during teaching courses to all ages of learners. After such a long period of fashionable disfavour there are many facts to learn which were taken for granted by women in a more leisurely age who all plied their hooks and knew the tricks from A to Z.

Crochet has changed since then, has lost its stuffy and time-consuming image and is now bold and exciting. There's no great merit in producing large slabs of it unless at the same time you acquire a foreign language

from the radio or something equally useful. But to use the craft
intelligently and discriminately can give attractive results without
involving a great deal of toil and time.

I am grateful to the Coats Sewing Group for their permission to
reproduce Figures 1 to 7 and to Mrs Beulah Allan for her help with the
diagrams.

1 Crochet know-how

It was in 1847 that *The Illuminated Book of Needlework* appeared with some space given to crochet, but it was not until the following year that the first complete crochet book was published, *My Crochet Sampler* by Miss Lambert. Her first name remains a decorous Victorian secret.

Much later, as the craft became popular in Europe, other books were produced in France and Germany, and by the end of the century as the demand increased several were available. Those were not the days of prolific publications for women and the single leaflet pattern, as we know it, was unheard of.

Since this almost forgotten craft was gradually reinstated and insinuated into top fashion in the early 1960s, leaflets and books have begun to appear, warily at first but now in large numbers, and the beginner has a wide choice of excellent instruction books. Crochet is not only one of the easiest and pleasantest of crafts but considering the time spent on it, one of the most effective.

Even so, as with most things, it is necessary to practise at first, to know the basic stitches, to know how to turn at the end of a row, how to increase and decrease and how to work in rounds. These basic rules should be absorbed until they become automatic—until you don't have to pause and wonder why that nice rectangle you started has dwindled into a tapering triangle or why the once flat circle has developed fluting at its perimeter or has caved in like a teacup.

So, if you are a novice, make squares in the basic stitches, rounds too, until almost without thinking you produce perfect samples. They need not be wasted; there are always little girls wanting dolls' blankets or aunts requiring kettle-holders. Or simply pull them out and start again!

The stitches

Chain stitch (ch)

This is the 'casting-on' stitch. It is also used in patterns where an open-work effect is required. A length of chain takes roughly four times as much yarn as the finished chain. If no edging is to be applied to the work, a firmer edge is made by starting with double yarn. So for a double chain allow eight times the length. Always leave about 6 in (15 cm) at the beginning of the chain. This can then be used to start sewing the seams, if any, eliminating the joining of yarn at the beginning of the seam.

If a long chain is to be made, don't count the stitches but make an approximate length. It is easier to count when working the first row of pattern. Any chain left over can be unpicked later. Each chain consists of three threads; the hook should always take up the two top ones. This

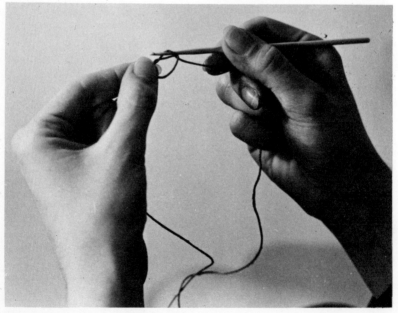

Plate 1a   Making a slip loop

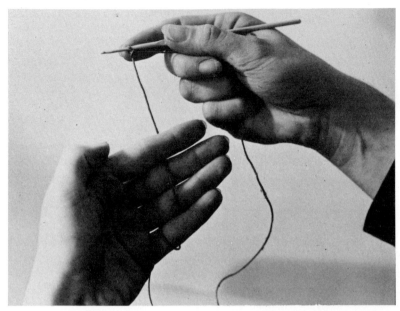

Plate 1b   Correct position of thread and hook before starting

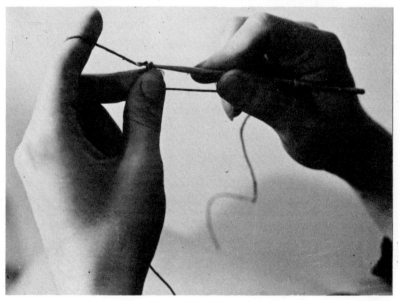

Plate 1c   Correct position of thread and hook for starting chain stitch

Fig 1   Chain stitch (ch st)

rule applies whenever working into the basic chain and almost always to
the two top threads of all stitches unless otherwise stated. Sometimes to
achieve a lacy or ridged pattern, only one thread is taken up, either the
back or the front one.

Slip stitch (ss)

This is the shallowest stitch, very flat, the shortest in height of all
crochet stitches. Not normally used as a fabric stitch but for joinings,
working across the top of stitches at armhole shapings and for making a
firm edge.

To work   With 1 loop on hook, insert hook under the next stitch, wool
over hook (woh), pull loop through stitch and loop on hook in one
movement. This produces a chain stitch on top of work.

Fig 2   Slip stitch (ss)

Make sample squares in the following stitches, using double knitting wool and a No 7 (4·50-mm) hook. There's no 'casting-off' stitch in crochet—just stop when you come to the end—or to perfection.

Double crochet (dc)

This is a strong firm stitch which results in a horizontal rib, two rows completing a rib.

To work   Make a length of 21 ch. Insert hook under two top threads, woh, draw loop through (2 loops on hook). Woh, draw loop through both loops on hook (1 loop on hook). 1 stitch completed.

Fig 3   Double crochet (dc)

To turn   Turn work round so that worked piece is on the left. 1 ch
(height of stitch). Miss first dc, work dc in second st and to end of row.
Finally work 1 dc into turning ch of previous row.

To increase   Make the first st into the two top threads as usual. Make a
second st into the back thread only of the same st. This method prevents
a large hole made with two stitches in one.

To decrease   Do not miss a stitch! Work 1 dc without drawing the
final loop through, but leaving 2 loops on hook. Work the next dc in the
same way, making 3 loops on hook. Woh, draw a loop through all loops
on hook, making two stitches into one.

Variations   A ridged effect is made by working into either the front or
back thread of the two top threads. This is sometimes specified in
pattern.

Half treble (htr)

A slightly higher stitch than double crochet, but still making a firm
fabric.

To work   Make a length of 22 ch. Miss 2 ch, woh, insert hook under 2
top threads of next ch, woh, draw loop through (3 loops on hook). Woh,
draw loop through all 3 loops on hook. 1 stitch completed.

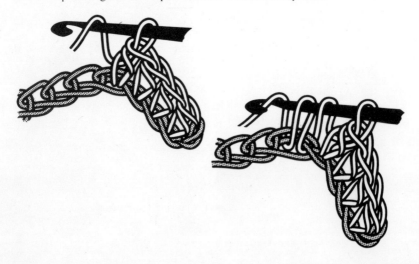

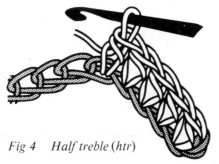

Fig 4   Half treble (htr)

To turn   Turn work as in dc instruction. 2 ch (height of stitch), miss first htr, work htr into second st and to end of row. Work last htr into turning ch of previous row.

To increase   Work 2 sts into 1, using same method as in dc, i.e. work second htr into back thread only.

To decrease   Woh, draw loop through next st, woh, draw loop through 2 loops on hook, woh, draw loop through next st, woh, draw loop through all 4 loops on hook.

Treble (tr)

A tall stitch, equivalent to three of four rows of knitting, so work grows quickly. Not such a firm fabric as those made with dc and htr, but probably the most commonly used stitch in crochet and many variations are possible.

To work   Make a length of 23 ch. Miss 3 ch, woh, draw loop through 2 top threads of next ch (3 loops on hook), woh, draw loop through 2 loops on hook, woh, draw loop through remaining loops. 1 stitch completed.

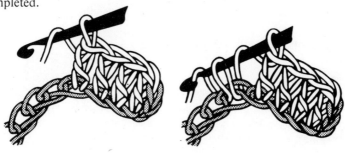

Fig 5   Treble (tr)

To turn   Turn work as before, 3 ch (height of stitch). Miss first tr, work tr into second st and to end of row. Work last tr into turning ch of previous row.

To increase   Work 2 sts into 1, but work second st into back thread only.

To decrease   Woh, draw loop through next st, woh, draw loop through 2 loops on hook, woh, draw loop through next st, woh, draw loop through 2 loops on hook, woh, draw loop through 3 loops.

Variations   These are infinite and many patterns are based on the treble stitch. Try 'v' stitch, making first a length of 23 ch and 1 row in trebles.

2nd row: 3 ch to turn, miss first st, * work 2 trs in next, miss next st. Rep from *. End with 1 tr. Turn.

3rd row: 3 ch, * miss first st, work 2 tr between 2 tr of previous 'v'. Rep from *. The second row can again be varied by working the 'v' (2 tr) into the top of either the first or second tr of previous row. For your first fancy stitch, try 1 row of tr and 1 row of 'v', alternately.

Double treble and triple treble (dtr and ttr)

These are elongated forms of the treble, made by passing yarn twice round the hook for double and thrice for triple, at the beginning of the stitch. The loops are worked off two by two, making tall stitches. Turning is made with 4 and 5 ch respectively (height of stitches), and basic rules for trebles apply.

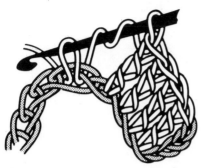

Fig 6   Double treble (dtr)

NB   *Turn* with the number of ch equivalent to the height of stitch.

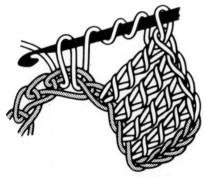

Fig 7   Triple treble (ttr)

Miss the first st, work to the end, finishing with a stitch in the turning ch of the previous row.

Then the edges remain straight!

Working in rounds

There are two methods. Working in a spiral in ever-increasing circles, or completing each round by joining with a slip stitch and starting again. The second method is more suitable when making rounds in different stitches and colours, the first when only one colour is to be used. Round pieces of crochet have many uses, from buttons to bathmats, though gone are the days when a good hostess graced her tea-table with delicately crocheted doilies, circular table-centres and tablecloths. Patterns for these are now museum pieces, astonishing in their intricacy and in the amount of time and patience required in their making.

Working in a spiral

Make 4 ch, join with ss to make a ring. Work 12 tr into the ring, working also over the starting end of wool—an easy way to dispose of it! When you reach the first tr, mark its position with a thread, showing the end of the round, but continue in tr without a break, carrying thread into successive rounds. Now increase in every other stitch for two further rounds, by which time your circle will be growing. The larger the circle the less frequent the increasing, and every other row can be worked without any increase. Your object is now to keep the circle flat. By the 6th row the increasing will be at every 6th stitch. This can be continued *ad infinitum*, but break off after about 8 rows and use it for a pot-holder!

Working in rounds

Make 6 ch, join with ss to form a circle. Make 12 dc into this, working over the starting end of wool. Join with ss to first dc.

2nd round: 1 ch (height of stitch), dc into first st, 2 dc into next. (Remember rule for increasing.) Repeat all round. Join with ss.

3rd round: As second.

4th round: Increase in every 4th st.

5th round: Work without increasing.

Work subsequent rounds with less frequent increases, e.g. in the 6th round increase every 6th st. By then every other round may be worked without any increase. The aim is to make a flat circle and you become the best judge of frequency of increasing. Avoid frilliness. Whatever stitch is used, start each round with number of ch equivalent to height.

To decrease   Follow the rule given for basic stitches.

Working in rounds of different colours

Finish each round, joining with ss. When ready to start another colour, break off wool and sew it in. Then start new and each subsequent colour at a *different position on the circle*. This avoids a repetition of joins in the same line from the centre.

Some problems explained

Q.   How do I alter tension?

A.   Commercial patterns usually state tension, i.e. numbers of stitches
and rows to stipulated measurements. It is wise to try out a sample,
otherwise your garment may be the wrong size. Make a 4-in (10-cm) or
6-in (15-cm) square with size of hook and wool as suggested in the
pattern. If you work too loosely, i.e. if your sample is bigger than it
should be, change to a hook one or two sizes smaller. A larger-size hook
should be used if your sample is too small. It is not easy to change your
personal tension to order!

Q.   How do I join wool in crochet?

A.   When only a short end remains, and working if possible on the
right side, make one stitch from the new ball and one from the old,
alternately for several stitches. Continue with the new ball, afterwards
darning in the ends. Or, the wool may be joined with a knot, leaving
ends long enough to be sewn in to the fabric. Afterwards undo the knot
and sew in the ends.

Q.   And how do I join seams?

A.   Crochet is a thick fabric and a seam can be clumsy. Also it is a
series of horizontal lines which should meet evenly at the seam.
Therefore, the best method is to lay the two pieces to be joined, right
side up, on a table. Then with a tapestry needle and matching yarn, draw
the edges together closely and invisibly with a stitch going from one
edge to the other, matching each horizontal line of stitch or pattern.

Q.   Often a sleeve top, if worked in pattern, has a serrated or scalloped
edge. How can this be sewn in neatly?

A.   Make a smooth edge with a row of dc all round the top. Or
alternate dc and ss, depending on the 'jaggedness' of the edge. Armholes
too, can be tidied up in this way before sewing in the sleeve.

Q.   What about pressing?

A.   Very little. The charm of crochet is in its raised stitch and rough surface. This can be spoiled by over-pressing.

On a soft surface such as a folded blanket, use a damp cloth and a warm iron lightly pressing the crochet into shape rather than flattening it. Pinning in shape to the blanket is useful. But beware pressing man-made yarns at all, nothing will bring up the pile once pressed.

Q.   Can I use different types of plys of wool and yarn when, for example, making motifs?

A.   It is not advisable to use man-made yarns with wool. Eventually the synthetic yarn will wear out the wool.

If you are using up oddments to make motifs, including double knitting and 3-ply wools, use two strands of 3-ply together. The aim should be to keep the fabric to an even thickness. You can add interest using two colours together.

Thick wools may be used for the centre of a motif, but subsequent rounds should be worked in wools of even thickness.

Q.   Is it possible to make darts in crochet?

A.   This is simple. In making a skirt, for example, having reached the position where darts should start, measure an even distance from centre back or front and mark the point of each dart. This will vary, obviously, but for an average size, front darts are approximately 4 in (10 cm) from centre and back darts 5 in (12·5 cm). Mark with coloured thread the point of each dart. All decreases should be made on the right side.

Work along to the threads and decrease 1 st at each one. The next row is worked without decreasing. Decrease in the next row and every other row for a depth of about 5 in (12·5 cm) or until the correct waist size is achieved.

A princess-shaped dress may be darted in the same way, decreasing from hips to waist and increasing again towards bust-line.

Plate 2   Crochet fabric with darts

Q. Ribbon-binding is often used to prevent the 'button' front of a jacket from stretching. Is there a less conspicuous method?

A. Yes. With tapestry needle and wool, start at the top button on the wrong side and work a chain stitch as far as the bottom one. This prevents stretching and is almost invisible.

Q. If making a raglan garment, can one achieve a 'fashioned' effect at the seam?

A. Yes, by consistently decreasing three stitches from the edge on both sleeve edges and back and front sections. The decreasing makes a symmetrical pattern.

Plate 3   Raglan sleeve in crochet

2 Edgings and trimmings

Edwardian days were supposedly golden and leisurely. Domestic labour was still cheap and plentiful. It was certainly not done to go out to work, and except for a very few of the higher-educated, the days of voluntary work for women, sitting on committees, attending women's meetings or even spending an afternoon round a bridge-table, had not yet arrived. As for encroaching on men's territory in the world of industry and commerce, hands would have been raised in horror at the thought. Those hands, instead, turned very often to crochet and long hours were whiled away in this refined occupation.

The result was that Edwardian homes were handsomely embellished with crochet which was used to decorate everything possible and more. An Edwardian housewife would trim most of her linen, towels, sheets and pillowcases, window-blinds and curtains. And, of course, valances for her dignified high beds, white linen hangings with deep crochet borders which successfully hid the box containing her best hat, dust and anything else which might have lurked in such a convenient hiding-place. Great pride was taken in heavily-trimmed table linen, cloths and tray cloths, mats and doilies, on which years of work were lovingly expended.

For her person, she would have her 'best handkerchiefs', used for more stately occasions, fine hand-drawn linen, crochet-edged; and crochet trimmings on both outer and under-wear. White cambric knickers with a 2-in border round the knees, crochet-edged petticoats and elaborate yokes on camisoles and nightdresses. Patterns were often sacrosanct and anyone having the temerity to ask for one might receive the reply, 'No, we like to keep *that* one in the family,' just as they kept private their favourite cake recipes.

Reaching further back into history, literally miles of crochet lace edgings were produced by the Carmelite nuns in Ireland from the mid-nineteenth century onwards and sold for their cause. They developed a

technique of their own, with raised flowers and leaves and designs based
on ecclesiastical architecture, and the Irish lace-making schools became
world-famous. Examples of this specialised crochet lace can be seen at
the Victoria and Albert Museum in London. To see them makes one feel
vaguely guilty about the way one's leisure is spent today.

Crochet edges still enhance church linen and the chasubles of clergy—a
superb one was noticed at the investiture of the Prince of Wales in
1969—but few people do such fine work today. It was probably the
First World War which put a stop to such activity, when knitting khaki
comforts became the necessary occupation for housewives. Since
then, fine crochet has gradually ceased to be in vogue as a craft in this
country. But crochet trimmings did return in an unexpected way when,
almost twenty years ago, Coco Chanel introduced her smart little suits
with crocheted and braided edgings which have since become classic.
Few, if any of us, get near enough to a Chanel suit to see the detail, but I
would like to suggest an easy and effective method for 'trimming the
edges'. There's a great sameness about wool jersey and man-made jersey
suits which are turned out by the million nowadays, stereotyped in
design. They can be given individuality and interest with a crochet
trimming. Similarly, that wilting suit that you're tired of can be given
new life and colour, while pinafore dresses, children's simple styles and
even coats will benefit from an original crochet edge.

Colours and materials

Colours can be matching or in contrast; wools, too, can be varied. Self-colour to match material gives a discreet edging; contrasts in one or two colours can be bold and interesting. For a smooth and neat edge on jersey materials, 3-ply wool is best, and a rough tweedy effect results when using a mixture or crinkled wool, obtainable in plain colours and variegated. On jacket and dress or trousered evening outfits, often in lurex woven material, an edging crocheted in one of the pretty lurex yarns is decorative; in fact, a little thought and imagination and not very much toil will result in clothes which are personal and distinctive.

Preparing the edges

Apart from loosely woven tweeds, most materials are too firm for the crochet hook to penetrate, yet it is essential for a smooth appearance that the edging should be worked *on* the garment. Sewn-on edgings look clumsy. The simple solution is to embroider the edge to be trimmed, in chain stitch with crewel needle and fine wool, e.g. 3-ply. This becomes the equivalent of the 'casting-on' chain, but is firmly attached to the garment.

Pattern suggestions

Using a No 9 hook (3·50 mm) which will slip easily into the chain-stitch edge, work 1 row in dc. This will give a firm foundation. After that, any simple stitch variation is used, and of course any width can be made.

Corners, as for example on collars and lapels, are kept sharp by working 3 sts into the corner ch space, and at inner corners the sts are decreased.

Try out any of the following on a short strip of material and decide on the most suitable for your purpose. Or, invent an edging yourself!

1   Working on the right side, make 1 row dc.

With a second colour, and working on the wrong side, make another row dc. The reverse side of the dc stitch gives an interesting effect.

2   *Corded edge*   Row 1: Dc.

Row 2: Working from left to right, instead of from right to left, work in dc, always inserting hook under both horizontal threads. This gives a serrated or corded edge.

3   Row 1: Dc, turn with 3 ch.

Row 2: * 2 trs into 2nd sp, miss 1 sp, rep from *.

A matching or contrasting fine ribbon or rouleau of chiffon can be threaded through the 'v' stitches.

4   As above, then working with another colour and working on the wrong side, 1 row dc.

5   Row 1: Dc, turn with 2 ch.

Row 2: Filet st. * 1 htr, 1 ch, miss 1 sp, rep from *.

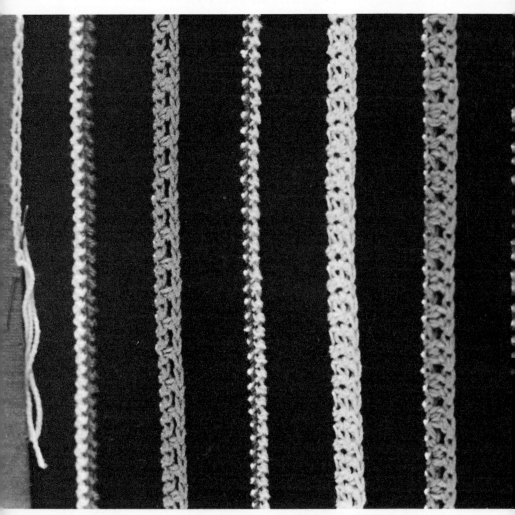

Plate 4   Some examples of edgings and trimmings. On the extreme left is a method of preparing the edge with chain stitch

6   Row 1 and 2 as above.

Row 3: Stretch corded edge in contrast. A cord st made over every ch sp worked loosely.

7   Row 1: Dc.

Row 2: 1 dc, 1 tr, into first sp, miss 1 sp, rep. Turn with 1 ch.

Row 3: * 1 dc, 1 tr into dc st of previous row, miss tr sp, rep from *. This is a firm and pretty stitch, can be made any width, suitable for a coat.

NB   For wider edgings, rows 2 and 3 should be repeated to the required depth then finished with a corded or picot edge.

8   *Picot edge*   * Ss into 3 sts, 1 dc into next st, 3 ch, 1 dc into same st as last dc, rep from *.

Trimming and making pockets

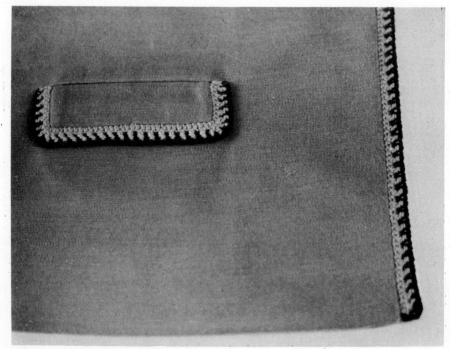

Plate 5   Crochet-trimmed flap pocket

If there are pockets on the garment you have edged, it is consistent to trim them similarly. The top of a welt pocket can be given a trim. If you have flap pockets with square corners, keep these sharp by working 3 sts into the corner ch. If rounded, an extra 1 or 2 sts on the curve will suffice. Sew the ends of the crochet invisibly to the garment.

Sometimes even phoney pockets make an additional trimming. An earnest dressmaker would frown at these, but where real pockets are impossible, these are the answer.

Crochet flap pocket

Usually $4\frac{1}{2}$ to 5 in long, 2 in deep.

Make a ch the required length, then work in pattern similar to the edging for 2 in. If any material is available, a narrow binding round three sides will give firmness. Or, if your edging has a corded edge, finish three sides with this and line the flap with silk to give weight.

Plate 6   Crochet flap pocket

Sew firmly to garment along the crochet edge.

Crochet patch pocket

Again if material is available—and sometimes straight strips can be cut from a shortened skirt hem—a crochet patch pocket with an edging of material gives importance.

Make a square of crochet to match edging with the top suitably finished.

Then cut three $1\frac{1}{2}$-in strips of material, equal to the size of the square plus turnings. Join together with mitred corners and sew to three sides of the crochet. Press. Now with a ruler measure an even distance from the join, of approximately $\frac{3}{4}$ to 1 in, marking with chalk or cotton. Turn in by this mark and press. Line with silk and slip stitch to garment.

Plate 7   Crochet patch pocket

Buttons to match

Covered in crochet to match a crochet or crochet-trimmed garment, these are an appropriate finish. The shiny appearance of bought ones, however pretty, is inconsistent, and though more time is involved in covering, the ultimate result is correct. Assuming that you have a collection of such things—and most craftswomen hoard everything which they think might be useful some day—you can often find suitable sizes and numbers of buttons for your purpose. If you haven't, then buy cheap buttons in the required size, but not wooden button moulds, which are heavy. Flat or slightly domed ones are best. The photograph shows some variations which are described here and general instructions are as follows:

1 If the button is shiny, cover first with material to match your wool. This will eliminate any gleam showing through the finished product.

2 If using 3-ply wool, use a No 12 (2·50-mm) hook. If a thicker wool, use a finer hook than that used on the garment. A firm tight stitch is necessary as the crochet covering will be stretched over the button.

3 Read again instructions for 'Working in rounds' on page 20 for increasing instructions.

Simple button worked in dc

Start with 3 ch, join with ss.

Round 1: 1 ch, 6 dc, join.

Round 2: 1 ch, 2 dc into each dc, join.

Round 3: 1 ch, * 2 dc, 2 dc into next dc. Rep from *, join.

Round 4: 1 ch, 1 dc into each dc, join.

Repeat round 4 until cover is almost the diameter of button, then decrease every other st for 2 rounds. Break off wool, thread needle with end and draw up edge. Insert button and fasten off securely.

Plate 8   Crochet-covered buckle and an assortment of crochet buttons

VARIATIONS

1   Turn the cover inside out and use the wrong side for the outside.

2   After inserting button, sew a chain stitch round the outer edge in contrasting colour.

3   A two-coloured button can be made by working the first 3 rounds in one colour and the rest in a contrast.

4   A decorative button, e.g. for an evening coat, can have sequins, pearls or beads sewn to the centre

Beehive buttons

Small beehive buttons are often more suitable than flat ones. Though excruciating to make, they're worth the trouble. The beehive effect is achieved by working into the back strand of the dc stitches.

Using a No 12 (2·50-mm) hook, make 3 ch and join.

Now working in a spiral, i.e. not joining each round, make 4 dc into ring and continue working into the back of stitches only, increasing slightly to get the domed shape. Try it over the tip of your first finger for size and shape. Break off when required size—about $\frac{1}{2}$ in in diameter and height (though this can be varied). Stuff with wool or cotton wool and draw up stitches at base.

The ring button

Less solid than the others, this button seems to merge unobtrusively into the crochet fabric. Yet it is quite practical and easily made. Those with long memories will remember how elaborate variations were made for use on hand-made garments in fine cambric or lawn, each button a work of the seamstress's art. I make this using a tapestry needle with a length of wool, and suggest this method. Using a ring of bone, metal or plastic in required size and 1 yard of wool for a $\frac{3}{4}$-in diameter, tie one end to ring, thread needle with other end and blanket stitch firmly and closely over the ring and over the short end of wool. When a quarter of the ring is covered, pass wool across to opposite side and back, twisting it two or three times over the first strand. Hold this in position while continuing the stitching over the next quarter, then pass wool over ring, thus making a cross in the centre. Twist again. Stitch remaining half of ring and return wool to centre of cross and sew round the eight strands. Leave end of wool for sewing on to garment eventually.

Petal buttons

These pretty little buttons are effective on rather 'dressed-up' clothes especially when made in a lurex mixture. If decorative buttons are wanted, these could be the answer.

Use a basic two- or four-holed button, $\frac{3}{4}$- to 1-in (2·5-cm) diameter and a No 12 hook (2·50 mm).

Make 9 ch and join.

Round 1: 18 dc. Join

Round 2: 1 dc into each dc.

Round 3: As round 2.

Round 4: Dec every other st.

Round 5: Dc, break off wool, leaving enough to draw through edge, insert into button and fasten off.

THE PETALS

Make 3 ch, join into ring. Then into ring make 1 dc, 2 tr, 1 dc, 5 times. Ss to first dc. Sew into button.

CENTRE

Make 2 ch. Insert hook into first ch, 3 times, drawing through $\frac{1}{4}$-in loops, woh, draw through all loops, ss. Pass ends through button and fasten off.

Covering a buckle

It's very easy to go and buy a buckle, but just as crochet buttons look best on a crochet dress or coat, so do buckles, covered likewise. If you haven't a suitable one in hoard, buy a dull-surfaced one, e.g. leather. If yours is shiny, bind round the outer edge with bias material to match your wool. The middle spoke will be covered by the belt.

Using a fine hook, No 12 (2·50 mm), make a ch the length of the inner edge, measured tightly. Join in a circle and work 1 row dc. If the buckle is rectangular, increase 1 st at the approximate position of the corners in the first and second rows. The number of rows to be worked depends on the width of the edge but as the crochet is stretched over the shape, it is advisable to make the entire cover on the small side. Decrease at the same points in the next rows which will cover the back. Break off, fit the crochet over the buckle and sew front and back together at the inner edge.

If your buckle is circular, work as above, increasing slightly in second and third rows, then decreasing.

A very narrow-edged buckle can be covered with needle and wool as described in 'The ring button'.

NB   Making a belt is described on page 144.

Flower trimmings

Raised flowers and leaves incorporated in the patterns were a feature of Irish crochet lace. Some of us like to read about them even if we haven't time to do them. There's a comprehensive collection of crochet books at the Victoria and Albert Museum in London dating back to 1847. Look at them if you're there. If not, watch junk and second-hand shops for any old books on crochet. They're worth snapping up for the ideas and historical interest they contain.

Snap up too, if you like collecting, pieces of old crochet which sometimes appear on market stalls. It's doubtful if you'll ever see their like again, and if you'll ever do anything as intricate. Apart from their value, which increases with the years, a collector gets real pleasure from just having them.

Returning then to modern times, you might like to spark up an evening outfit with crochet flowers. And as originality is important for a wedding dress, I can imagine white and lurex crochet flowers making a charming trimming.

Here, then, are instructions for basic flowers and leaves from which variations may be made.

Flower 1

Using a No 12 (2·50-mm) hook and 3-ply wool, or finer, make 6 ch and join into circle. Into it make (5 ch 1 dc) 5 times.

Into each loop make 2 dc, 5 tr, 2 dc.

Working from the back and into the original circle, make (1 dc 7 ch) 5 times.

Into each loop make 2 dc, 7 tr, 2 dc.

Again into original circle put (1 dc 9 ch) 5 times.

Into each loop make 2 dc, 9 tr, 2 dc.

This gives you 15 petals and a flower about 2 in across, which is probably big enough for most purposes.

Flower 2

Flat and very simple, suitable for neck and sleeve decoration.

Hook and wool as above.

Make 3 ch and join. Into ring put 12 dc, join with ss.

* 6 ch, turn. 1 dc in 5th ch, 4 tr in next 4 ch, ss to 2nd dc of centre ring *. Rep from * to * 5 times, joining each petal to alternate dcs in ring. Finally, ss all round edge of petals. Contrasting colour may be used.

Leaf 1

Hook and wool as above.

Make 9 ch, turn.

Miss 1 ch, then 1 dc, 1 htr, 4 tr, 1 htr, 1 ss.

Now work up the other side of the ch: 1 ss, 1 htr, 4 tr, 1 htr, 1 ss. Join at the top with another ss. Break off and sew in end.

Leaf 2

Make 10 ch, turn.

Miss 1 ch, then 1 ss, 3 dc, 3 tr, 2 dc, 1 ch, turn.

Work up the other side of ch: 2 dc, 3 tr, 3 dc, 1 ss.

Now work ss all round leaf, but working into the top thread only of previous row.

NB   The outer petals of Flower 1 and the leaves may be stiffened by
laying a piece of fuse wire along the edge of each and working a row of
dc over it.

Edelweiss flower

A flat flower trimming which can be used as a separate motif or can be
joined together to form an edge for sleeves or neckline.

Required: choice of wool and appropriate hook.

Make 3 ch, join with ss.

10 dc into centre, join with ss to ch.

1 ch, 1 tr into first sp, 1 dtr, 1 tr into 2nd sp.

* 1 dc, 1 tr into 3rd sp, 1 dtr, 1 tr into 4th sp *.

Rep from * to * 3 times, making 5 petals, join with ss.

Break off wool leaving 12 in. Thread into tapestry needle and oversew
round outer edge, making 1 st into every sp and 2 sts into each dtr sp.
Fasten off, press lightly.

Cords and braids

Triangular braid

A strong and decorative braid with various uses. Makes excellent bag handles when bought ones might be unsuitable; can be made into a belt with adhesive tape backing, or used wherever a braid finish is required. For bag handles, nylon yarn gives hard wear.

Make a chain the required length.

On it make 2 rows dc, then 1 row corded edging (see page 31).

Make another corded edge on the chain stitch side.

Pick up stitches in the centre of the dc rows, and make a third corded edge.

Twisted cord

A cord trimming is useful for finishing cushions and hats, used as a drawstring in a bag or simply as a belt for a dress. Make it in one colour or variegated.

Take several lengths of wool at least three times the length of cord required. Tie the ends into a knot and slip it over a hook. Holding the other end, twist round and round in the same direction until it is very tight. If you have a loop at this end, a pencil inserted will make twisting easier. Release from hook and let the two sides twist together. Undo the knot, bind round all ends to make a tassel. Cut ends even. The folded end can also be cut and tasseled, as required.

Bobbinette cord

Not crochet, but a useful means of involving the family. Children enjoy making a round cord on an empty cotton reel. Although it's more fun to make it in patches of different colours, if you can persuade your child (bribery?) to make it in one colour, she or he will produce a useful cord for finishing the edge of a cushion or for wearing on a dress. Stiffen it, if you like, by inserting a piping cord, tuck a tassel into each end or twist and sew the ends into a snail shape.

Making this is sometimes a long and laborious job, so get it started well ahead of schedule.

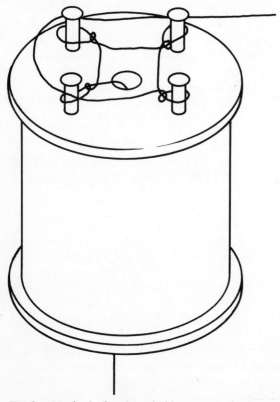

Fig 8   Method of making bobbinette cord using wooden cotton reel with four nails hammered in

Wooden cotton reels are gradually being replaced by others of less use—from our point of view, so hoard them. They have many uses where there are children.

You need an empty cotton reel with four round-headed nails hammered into the top. Wool of uniform thickness and thick tapestry needle.

Make a loop with a fairly long end which is inserted down the centre of the reel. Loop goes over first nail. With fingers knot three loops over the other nails. Lay wool round, and with needle lift the lower loops over the laid wool, working in a clock-wise direction. Pull wool end after each round.

Tassels

Wind wool round a piece of stiff cardboard cut the required length for tassel. Draw one end together using a tapestry needle, leaving ends for sewing. Cut the loops at other end, take off cardboard, wind wool round the top to form the tassel, cut the ends evenly with scissors.

Above: Detail of waistcoat/below: Detail of crochet-edged poncho

Above: Round cushion/below: One-square Afghan cushion

3 Motifs and making the most of them

Making motifs in large numbers for blankets and cot-covers is a fascinating hobby. One gets involved with the arrangement of colours, the scrounging of oddments of wool from friends and there's always the compulsion to make just one more to complete a section or to use up some scraps of wool. One of my friends, albeit a scrounger, times herself and swears she can do an Afghan in five minutes. While waiting for potatoes to come to the boil she knocks one off, hook and wools always at the ready in her overall pocket. Her blankets grow outrageously quickly.

To embark on a large bedspread in plain colour requires more of a pioneering spirit and much time and patience. You can, nowadays, have one made for you at a high but not exorbitant price. For about one-sixth of the price settle down to an endurance test.

This craft is not new. When, throughout the nineteenth century, waves of immigrants crossed the Atlantic to the New World, they took with them not only the culture of their countries but also the crafts. So it was that crochet patterns of intricacy and charm which had been used for generations in parts of Europe became eventually 'traditional American' and were used for making the beautiful cotton bed-covers which are a feature of many American homes. Books of patterns are available, the designs often bearing the name of the country of origin, and the craft today is as popular as it was a hundred years ago.

In this country, now that the novelty of man-made fabrics on our beds has worn off, we have begun to appreciate the appearance and lasting quality of cotton and the fashion for hand-made crochet covers is with us again.

But motifs do not stop at bedrooms, and their possibilities, now that fashion is so adventurous, are endless. Things to wear, even for men, and things to use are already making a gay impact, and with imagination and colour sense these can be quite beautiful. Cottage industries are cropping up. In several Bedfordshire villages everyone sufficiently able-bodied to wield a crochet hook is busy making motifs. Carefully chosen colour schemes are used and household goods and children's clothes in modern trend are made from them. Mrs McIndoe, who started this enterprising industry, is to be congratulated. Catalogues may be obtained from her at: 'Village Squares', Old Farm, Chalton, Luton, Bedfordshire. The traditional Afghan design which she uses, and several others in different shapes, are given in this chapter with suggested uses, but try making a chain ring and going from there! You may surprise yourself. And try out each motif in any available wools, then consider their application.

Points to observe

1   Never mix man-made fibres with pure wool or cotton. One would wear out the other. So, all synthetic or all natural.

2   Motifs should be of even texture. If necessary, use two strands of fine wool or cotton together to retain the same texture as other material used.

3   Blankets, pram covers, rugs, etc., should be reversible. Care should be taken to eliminate all ends and to finish off neatly.

Joining up

There are several methods, appropriate to different articles being made, and to different shapes of motif:

(*a*) Sew together with a tapestry needle, using wool left on end of motif. Sew through both top stitches of edge. Strong enough for garments.

(*b*) Over-sew through back loop of edge only. This leaves a decorative line round each motif and gives a very smooth finish. An embroidered star in contrasting colour can improve the centre join of every four motifs.

(*c*) Blankets, bedspreads and rugs get hard wear. Join motifs together with slip stitch or double crochet for strength.

Plate 9   Method of joining up four square motifs with embroidered star

(*d*) Motifs can be joined together during the course of the work. Complete one, then while working the last side of the second, make a chain stitch, insert hook into previous motif and work a slip stitch. Do this at each end and in the centre of square or rectangular motifs.

(*e*) When joining round or octagonal shapes, there is often a space left in the middle of four. This can be filled with a central star, joined to the outer motifs with slip stitch. Star: make ring of 3 ch. Now make points

in ch (number according to size of gap), joining the points to edges of
motifs, and each point finished at centre ring with ss.

Plate 10   Method of joining up round motifs with crochet star

The Afghan motif

The most usual, useful for using up oddments and for making up into cot-covers and blankets. A practical size for a cot-cover or what used to be called a 'sofa rug' and again fashionable, can be made by joining up 11 squares for the width and 19 squares for the length. This works out roughly at 36 by 60 in (91 by 150 cm). Surrounding edges of each motif and final border should be of the same colour; this blends the colourful galaxy of the centres into a design, and may be in any strong colour or white. Hook and wools are a matter of choice. Worked in blocks of 3 tr, the 3 ch at the beginning of each round counts as 1 tr. Trebles are worked into the spaces, not into the chain.

Method

Make 4 ch into a ring. (Each round starts with 3 ch, counted as the first tr.)

Round 1: 3 tr, 1 ch, 4 times, ss to top of first tr (i.e. 3 ch). Break off wool.

Round 2: Join on new colour at a ch sp, 3 tr, 1 ch, 3 tr in each of the 4 ch sps, ss, and break off wool.

Round 3: Join on a new colour at a ch sp. 3 tr, 1 ch, 3 tr in corner, 3 tr between grs. Rep 3 times. Join with ss, break off.

Round 4: The same as round 3, except that there will be two grs of 3 tr between each corner, finish as before.

This completes the motif though it may be made bigger by repetition, increasing the numbers of grs of 3 tr between each corner. (See 'One-Square' Afghan Cushion, page 117.)

Cotton bedspread

This is quickly made in heavy cotton, each square taking less than half an hour to work.

Each square measures 7 in (17·5 cm).

There are 10 squares in width, 15 squares in length.

Finished size of single bedspread is 70 by 105 in (178 cm by 2·5 m).

You will need

65 balls Coats Musica Health Cotton
Hook No 5 (5·50 mm)

Directions for square

6 ch, join in a ring with ss.

Round 1: 4 ch (=1 tr 1 ch), 1 tr 1 ch, 11 times. Join with ss to third ch, then ss to first sp.

Round 2: Puff stitch (p st). Woh, draw loop through first sp 3 times, woh, draw loop through all loops. 1 ch. Rep in every sp, ss to top stitch at beginning of round. (12 p sts.)

Round 3: 1 ch, 1 dc in top of first p st, 2 dc in sp. Rep to end of round, join with ss. (36 sts.)

Round 4: 4 ch, * 1 p st in first st, 1 ch, miss 1 st, 1 p st 1 ch, miss 1 st, 1 p st 1 ch, miss 1 st, 1 p st 1 ch, 2 tr in next st, 1 ch. 2 tr in next, Rep from * 3 times but omit last tr at end of round. Ss to third of 4 ch, which counts as second tr.

Round 5: 4 ch, 1 tr in first st before p st, 1 tr in top of p st, 1 tr in top of ch. Continue around with 1 tr in each st, and 2 tr, 1 ch, 2 tr in each corner ch sp. Join with ss in third of 4 ch.

Plate 11   Detail of bedspread made in heavy cotton

(Square of 15 trs, with 1 ch at corners.)

Round 6: 4 ch, miss first tr, * 1 tr 1 ch, miss 1 tr. Rep from * all round but working 2 tr, 1 ch, 2 tr, 1 ch, at each corner. Join with ss to third of 4 ch.

Round 7: 1 ch, 1 dc in ch sps, 1 dc in top of trs, all round. 3 dcs in corner ch sps. Join to 1 ch.

Round 8: 1 ch, turn work, and working on wrong side, make 1 dc in every st, 2 dcs in corner dc. Join with ss to 1 ch. Break off, leaving a length of yarn for sewing to next square.

Sew squares together on wrong side with an oversewing stitch, taking up the top thread of each edge stitch and being careful to keep seams as elastic as the crocheted fabric.

A fringe may be added on the two long sides and lower edge, but a two-row double crochet edge all round would be a more practical finish, enabling the bedspread to be turned from end to end.

Spectacle case

Plate 12   Spectacle case made in lurex and nylon mixture

If you have to carry spectacles, which so many of us do, carry them in an attractive case, different from the next one. This could be made to go with an evening dress, colour and material to match. Black lurex mixture is also good. The motifs are made in one colour, thus halving the making time, and as the work is turned at the completion of each round this also simplifies the operation.

The diagram shows the shape and size of the case, for which you will need the following small amounts:

A double piece of Vilene
A suitable piece of material for underlay of crochet (evening dress material?)
A piece of lining material
1 oz Robin Galaxie lurex and nylon mixture, and No 12 hook (2·50 mm)

The crochet

Make 4 Afghan squares, $2\frac{1}{2}$ in (6·5 cm).

Add 1 row tr to *one* side of each square. Sew in pairs across treble stitches making two panels, 6 by $2\frac{1}{2}$ in (15 by 6·5 cm).

Make a border of trebles on the two long sides and across one end, with 4 tr in each bottom corner. Join one side, then work across the top to give a curved finish 6 dc, 12 tr, 6 dc.

Rep once. Turn and work 2 rows dc. Press lightly.

Join up other side and bottom end, leaving the curved end open.

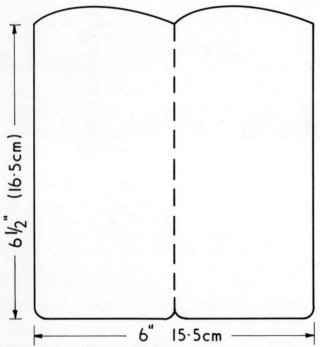

Fig 9   Pattern for spectacle case

The case

1   Draw and cut out pattern in paper.

2   Cut a double piece of Vilene, without turnings.

3   Cut one piece underlay and one piece lining with $\frac{1}{4}$-in (0·5-cm)
turnings.

4   Oversew the two curved edges of the two pieces of Vilene together,
fold lengthwise and oversew long sides and across bottom end.

5   Stitch lining and underlay together across curved top, $\frac{1}{4}$-in (0·5-cm)
turning, notch between curves. Spread out, fold lengthwise (right sides
together), stitch across end of underlay and long side, then long side
only of lining, taking a wider turning because this tucks inside the case.
Turn out and press.

6   Insert Vilene case into underlay, using a ruler to push into position.
Now make a $\frac{3}{4}$-in (2-cm) turning on end of lining and seam edges
together. Push into case. Tack around opening to hold in position.

7   Draw crochet over case, pin around top curve, making crochet
extend slightly over edge. Sew invisibly and firmly.

Finally, lay a strand of yarn over join of underlay and lining and couch
to neaten.

Hexagonal rug motif

Plate 13   Detail of rug showing arrangement of motifs: six main motifs surrounding a reverse motif with half motifs filling in spaces at end of rug

Less usual than the Afghan and perhaps with more interesting possibilities, this hexagonal motif may also be made from oddments or better still in a definite colour scheme. In that case, while the majority of the motifs are made shading from light to dark, this order may be reversed for centre motifs of groups of seven. See illustration.

Five colours are used, as follows:
Round 1: Colour 1
Round 2: Colour 2
Rounds 3 and 4: Colour 3

Round 5: Colour 4
Round 6: Colour 5

For a rug or blanket measuring 55 by 74 in (140 by 190 cm) approximately, you will need:

7 oz colour 1
7 oz colour 2
14 oz colour 3
10 oz colour 4
15 oz colour 5

All in 4-ply wool. Hook No 9 (3·50 mm).

Make 124 motifs as described below, 39 motifs with colours reversed, i.e. dark to light, and 12 half motifs in main colour. Arrange in groups (see Plate 13) with 6 motifs surrounding each reverse motif, and half motifs filling in spaces at each end of rug. Complete with 1 row of trs in main colour.

Making the motif

Make 5 ch and join into a ring.

Round 1: Into the ring work 3 ch, 2 tr (1 ch, 3 tr) five times making 6 grs, 1 ch, join to top of first 3 ch with ss. Join on 2nd colour.

Round 2: 3 ch, 1 tr in first ch sp between grs, (1 ch 2 tr) in same sp. * (2 tr, 1 ch, 2 tr) in next sp. Rep from * 4 times, ss, break off. (6 grs of 2 tr, 1 ch, 2 tr.)

Round 3: (3 ch, 1 tr) in non-chain sp, miss 2 tr, (2 tr, 1 ch, 2 tr) in centre of gr, miss 2 tr, 2 tr in next sp. Continue to end of round. Join with ss. The hexagon is now formed with grs of 2 tr, 1 ch, 2 tr at 6 points.

Round 4: Ss to next sp, then work as for round 3 but with 2 grs of 2 trs between each point. Ss and break off.

Round 5: Same as round 3 but with 3 grs of 2 trs between each point.

Round 6: Same as round 3 but with 4 grs between each point. Ss, break off, leaving an end for sewing.

Making a half motif

Using one colour throughout, make a ring of 3 ch.

Round 1: 3 ch, 1 tr, 1 ch, 3 tr, 1 ch, 2 tr, 3 ch, turn.

Round 2: 1 tr in top of last tr, miss 1 tr, (2 tr, 1 ch, 2 tr) in next ch sp, 1 ch, miss 3 tr, (2 tr, 1 ch, 2 tr) in next ch sp, miss 1 tr, 2 tr in turning ch, 3 ch, turn.

Round 3: 1 tr in top of last tr, miss 1 tr, 2 tr in next sp, * miss 2 tr, (2 tr, 1 ch, 2 tr) in next ch sp, miss 2 tr, 2 tr in end ch sp. Rep from * once, miss 1 tr, 2 tr in top of turning ch, 3 ch, turn.

Rounds 4, 5, and 6: Continue in pattern with pairs of 2 trs between points.

Another hexagonal

A useful shape, this one, as its six straight sides will join with others into a circle. It can be increased in size by repeating the last row, forming a solid frame-work to a brightly coloured centre. Is effective made in thick wool, suitable for a child's or adult's skirt. Use any wools of uniform thickness and corresponding hook.

Method

Make 3 ch. Join.

Row 1: 3 ch, 23 tr (making 24 tr). Join on second colour.

Row 2: 1 dc, 4 ch, miss 1 st. Rep making 12 loops. Join.

Row 3: 1 dc, 2 htr, 1 dc, in each loop. Join on 3rd colour.

Row 4: * 5 tr, in 2nd htr of previous row, 3 ch, 1 dc in 2nd htr of next scallop, 3 ch *. Rep from * to *. Join.

Row 5: * 5 dc into each of 5 tr, 3 ch, 1 dc into next dc, 3 ch, rep from *. Join.

Row 6: Join on 4th colour. Starting at a dc between chs in previous row make * 1 dc, 2 dc in 3 ch of previous row, 1 dc, 1 htr, 2 tr in 1 dc, 1 htr, 1 dc, 2 dc in 3 ch. Rep from * 5 times.

Row 7: Make dc in every st, and 2 dc between trs at the six points of hexagon. (This last row may be repeated, as suggested above.)

The shopping bag

Plate 14a   Bag covered with hexagonal motifs

The bag illustrated was an old shopping bag with stiff cardboard interior covered inside and out with lining material. Motifs were made and joined into a circle. A piece of felt cut the size of the base and extending $1\frac{1}{2}$ in up the sides of the bag was stuck on. The sewn-up motifs were stretched over the shape and at the lower edge were sewn to the felt.

The upper edge was straightened with 2 rows ss and tr, the ss worked along the top and the tr arranged to fill in the deeper spaces. This was sewn to the top of the bag and the handles attached.

Above: Floppety Flo and Brown Betty/below: Frilly Armadillo

Duffle bag

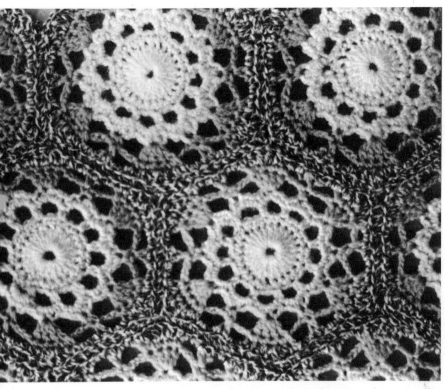

Plate 14b   Close-up of motifs showing method of joining

A duffle bag

Decorative and useful. Mine hangs from a hook screwed into a window-sill, holds all small oddments of wool and looks very pretty, too.

Plate 15   *Duffle bag covered with wide band of hexagonal motifs*

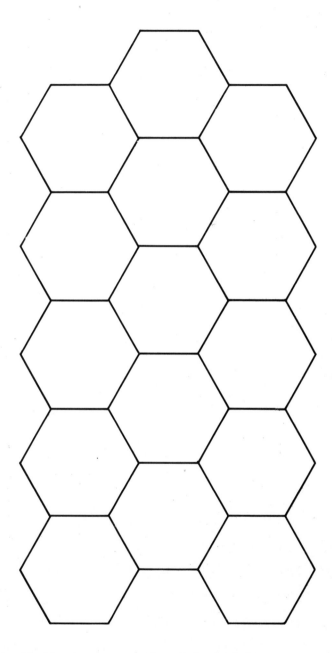

Fig 10   Arrangement of motifs for duffle bag

Make an attractive colour scheme for this, using up oddments of wool
for centres of motifs, but the same wool for all the outside edges. Lurex
yarn incorporated in the motifs adds to the appearance.

Size given in the diagram is for motifs measuring 4 by $3\frac{1}{2}$ in. A little
simple arithmetic will produce a larger or smaller bag. Use a plain but
strong furnishing or moygashel fabric in plain colour to tone with wool.

You will need

$\frac{1}{2}$ yd of either 36-in wide moygashel-type material or furnishing fabric
48 in wide
Oddments of wool for motifs, 1 oz main colour, all 4-ply
Cardboard base, 8-in diameter

Method

Cut material for bag and two bases and cut one base of cardboard as
shown in Fig 11. Stitch up side seam, making a tube. Turn inside out.
Pin this on one base and stitch on wrong side. Lay cardboard over base,
and hem second material base over it, covering join. Turn in $3\frac{1}{2}$ in at the
top, make casing $\frac{3}{4}$ in wide for cord, with two rows of machining, but
remember to leave opening for cord. Make 18 motifs from previous
pattern, sew together into a tube, stretch over bag, sew to material at top
and bottom edges.

Make a twisted or double chain cord in mixed wools and slot through
casing.

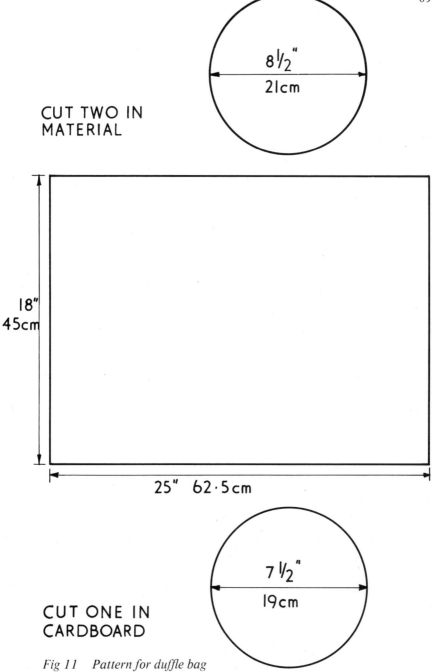

CUT TWO IN
MATERIAL

8½"
21cm

18"
45cm

25" 62·5cm

7½"
19cm

CUT ONE IN
CARDBOARD

Fig 11   Pattern for duffle bag

Swedish scalloped bag

Try this pattern, then make the bag described below.

Plate 16   Swedish scalloped bag made entirely of cotton

Use No 7 (4·50-mm) hook and double knitting wool.

Each round is joined with ss.

Make 8 ch, join.

Into this circle, work 24 tr (3 ch count as first tr). Join.

Then, (1 dc, 6 ch, miss 2 sps, 1 dc, 4 ch, miss 2 sps) 4 times. Join. (8 loops.)

In the big loops work 1 dc, 1 ch, 6 tr, 1 ch, 1 dc.

In the small loops work 1 dc, 1 ch, 2 tr, 1 ch, 1 dc, join.

A second motif can be joined to the first at two points in big loops and one point in small loops.

The bag

After their long dark winter the Swedes enjoy their hot summer days wearing bright clothes and accessories. Everything dreary and wintery is hidden away. The bag illustrated here is popular, fresh and washable, made entirely of cotton. A hand-bag size is given which can easily be enlarged to make a shopping bag.

You will need

3 balls White Vest Cotton
No 5 or 6 (5·50- or 5·00-mm) hook
Washable cotton lining in bright colour, $\frac{3}{8}$ yd
Bag handles

Method

Make 12 motifs, joining as described into 2 sets of six. Press. For gusset, crochet in dc a strip on 10 ch, 25 in (63 cm) long. Pin this to the edge of motifs starting 1 in (2·5 cm) from top edge. Sew with white cotton, running the needle through the edge of crochet from one point to the next. Pick up sts along the top of motif blocks and work in tr to form a straight edge. Then work two further rows of trs.

Now make lining for the bag, cutting paper pattern to size of crochet. Measure the 6-motif block, add 1 in (2·5 cm) at top and $\frac{1}{4}$ in (0·5-cm) turnings all round. Measure the gusset strip, add $\frac{1}{4}$-in (0·5-cm) turnings. Cut out in material. Cut a pocket piece, turn in and stitch along top edge, then stitch to one side of lining. Join gusset to sides, stitch and sew by hand into bag. Using a bag handle which has adaptable rods and screw ends, slot rods through top rows of trebles. Remove on washing day!

Quick-thick motif

Plate 17   Bag covered with motifs of different sizes

If you like quick results, try this one. It is effective because of the different wool textures and the bright colours used, and because the interest is in these features, the stitches are necessarily simple.

Use any variety of thick wools, e.g. double knitting, crêpe double knitting, crinkle-spun, in brilliant colours such as orange, bright pink and cherry, to produce a bold motif suitable for a large bag. See colour plate 3.

You will need

1 oz orange DK wool

1 oz pink DK crêpe wool
4 oz Cherry Crinkle-spun (or colours of choice)
No 7 (4·50 mm) hook, bag handle with slotting rods, 9 in (22·5 cm)
Underlay and lining. 10 large motifs

Method

THE MOTIFS

Orange   4 ch, join in a ring. 3 ch (counting as 1 tr) 11 tr. Join with ss.

Pink   1 dc, 2 ch, all round, working dcs between trs. Join, then ss to
first ch sp. 1 tr, 3 ch, in every 2 ch sp, all round. Join, then ss to centre
of ch sp.

Crinkle   2 tr, 3 ch, in every 3 ch sp. Join, then ss to centre of 2 trs. 1
dc, 5 ch in centre of trs and centre of 3 ch sp. Join.

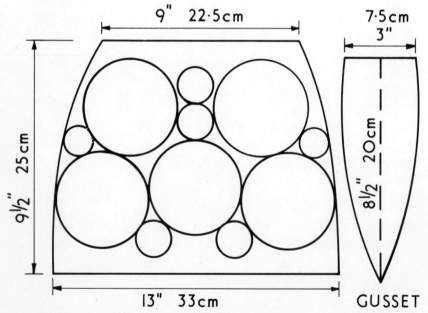

Fig 12   Pattern for handbag showing arrangement of motifs

The bag lining Cut paper pattern from diagram, then cut two bag shapes and two gussets from muslin or useful old sheets, and pin motifs to these as shown. Then make 12 small motifs from 1st and 2nd rows only, joining each to scallops of large motifs with 1 ch, 1 ss, during 2nd working row. When these are in position, using Crinkle-spun, fill in the gaps at top sides and bottom with dtrs and trs to complete the shape of the pattern. Remove from material and press very lightly: crinkly wool should not be flattened. Pin each side to underlay material, which should be cut with $\frac{3}{8}$-in (1-cm) turnings.

In Crinkle-spun make the two gussets to size of pattern, starting with 2 tr and increasing to 14 tr. Mount these on underlay material and sew to the sides of bag. Make lining from pattern and sew in, leaving edge of crochet at the top. Crochet a final row of tr across top of each side. Slot handle rods through these.

Square motif with round centre

This is made in four colours but might well be made in one.

1st row and colour: 6 ch, join in ring, 12 dc in ring, join with ss.

2nd row and colour: 3 ch (counting as first tr) 1 tr in first sp, 2 ch,
* miss 1 sp, 2 tr in next sp, 2 ch. Rep from * 4 times, making 6 'v' sts.
Join with ss.

3rd row: 1 dc between trs, 3 dc across 2 ch. Rep, join with ss.

4th row, 3rd colour: 3 tr in centre of 3 dc, 3 tr above 'v' st, 3 tr in centre
of 3 dc, 3 ch. Rep 3 times, making a square.

5th row, 4th colour: Start at a 3 ch corner. * (4 tr, 2 ch, 4 tr) in corner,
1 ch, 2 tr between 3 tr block, 1 ch, 2 tr between 3 tr block, 1 ch *. Rep
from * to * 3 times. Join.

6th row: Dc all round square, with 2 dc in each corner.

Use this motif for the waistcoat below.

Waistcoat with the western look

Colour plate 4 shows jersey material waistcoat with a border of these motifs and fringe. 5th and 6th rows, fringe and corded edge should match material.

To make the waistcoat

Using a pattern of your size, cut out in chosen material and in lining to match. Stitch darts, join side and shoulder seams of both material and lining. Press. Pin lining to material, right sides facing, and tack together round fronts and neck. Stitch, trim edges, notch back of neck, turn right side out and press. Turn in armhole edges on material, turn in lining similarly, and hem to material. Oversew raw edge of hem, turn up lining hem and sew to material $\frac{1}{4}$ in (0·5 cm) above.

Motifs

Now make motifs which when joined together will make border for lower edge. E.g. 11 motifs, each $3\frac{1}{2}$ in (9 cm) square, will edge a garment approx 38 in (98 cm) at the hem. Correct size can be manipulated by working additional rows dc round each motif if necessary.

Join motifs, lay on right side of waistcoat with the top edge covering the oversewn edge of material. Tack and sew to waistcoat through edge of motifs.

Cut 8-in (20-cm) lengths of wool for fringe, and using a hook and 4 strands knot tassels to lower edge of motifs, placing one at join and three spaced equally across motif—4 tassels to each motif.

With needle and wool, sew a chain stitch, i.e. embroidery stitch, on armhole edges and front and neck edges. Into this, crochet a corded edge (see page 31).

4 *The owl, the pussycat and other curious creatures*

Plate 18   The owl and the pussycat

This is a chapter for imaginative grandmothers, adoring aunts, busy mothers and those light-hearted people who enjoy making toys. Busy mothers are included because there is so little time involved, each section of crochet taking only a few minutes to do. The assembly of the toys is so easy and quick that even the busiest mother can tackle them cheerfully.

The toys are soft, cuddlesome and washable. They can be made from small oddments of wool in any colour or mixture of colours. The more outrageous and unreal the colouring, the more, seemingly, are toys appreciated nowadays. The linings may be made from used cotton or silk material and, given a crochet hook or two which presumably are in stock, the only expense is on the kapok or other stuffing, and a bag of that goes a long way.

The toys have been tried out on small children with complimentary results. In one case, a lifelong bedfellow, Ted, was ousted in favour of the owl. What greater reward could one wish for? Crochet stitches have descriptive names. Shell stitch and star stitch, pineapple and popcorn, triangle and check stitch, all of which inspire one's imagination. Curiously there's no feather stitch in crochet, but 'v' stitch worked in a fluffy cream wool resembles feathers, more so when turned upside down. That suggested the breast of a bird and the bird became an owl. And the owl was the beginning of the toys described in this chapter.

General instructions for all the toys

All are made in the same way. The linings are stitched and stuffed, the crochet sections are then made to cover the stuffed shape. Because edges of crochet are drawn together without seams (see page 22), it is unnecessary to allow turnings on the crochet sections. These are made to fit paper patterns, therefore *no turnings are allowed*. But turnings must be allowed when cutting the linings. Direction of crochet on each section is marked with arrows on the patterns.

Making the lining

1   Trace the pattern on to thin paper, then cut out in firm paper or thin cardboard.

2 Using cotton or silk material in appropriate colour, cut out, leaving $\frac{1}{2}$-in (1·5-cm) turnings.

3 Stitch with small but not tight machine stitches or backstitch by hand, leaving an opening for stuffing at the top of the head and at one end of the dolls' arms and legs.

4 Stuff quite firmly but not too hard, remembering that these are *soft* toys. Use a pencil or knitting needle to push stuffing into corners.

5 Sew up opening.

You now have the stuffed shape of the toy and the flat paper patterns. These are the guides to the size and shape of the crochet sections. It is now quite easy to make the crochet sections to fit the paper patterns, increasing and decreasing, following the shapes and any confident worker might like to work this out for herself. But working instructions are given for the sizes shown. These may be altered to suit thicker or finer wool, or for looser or tighter tension. More or less stitches will be required for any variation in size and the work should be checked over the pattern throughout.

To enlarge or reduce patterns

It is possible that you will be requested to produce a large mother owl or a small baby pussycat, especially after your first attempt. This being so, you will need to make the patterns larger or smaller. This is a simple operation.

Draw the patterns on squared paper. Then draw larger or smaller squares on another piece of paper and copy the patterns on to this, keeping the shape accurate in every detail.

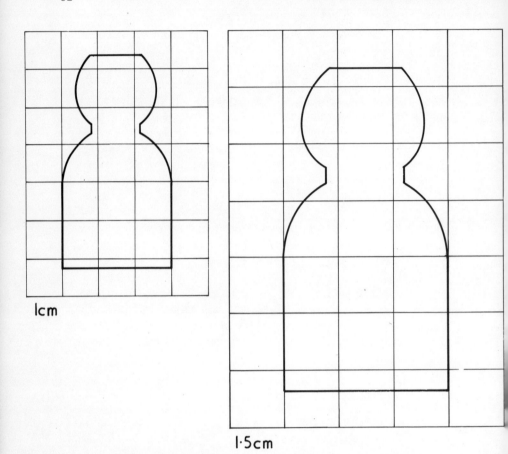

1cm

1·5cm

Fig 13   Enlarging a pattern

The owl

The original is made in owl-like colours, cream and brown, but this is a matter of choice. The finished article looks like an owl whatever colours are used, and a rummage through the oddment bag might produce some interesting and possibly startling combinations.

Mohair and wool, either a manufactured mixture or using strands of mohair and wool together gives a soft, fluffy appearance to the back and sides, while a flecked wool could be used for the front of the bird. The finished effect is not meant to be realistic after all.

You will need

A very small amount of cream or white double knitting
About $\frac{1}{2}$ oz brown, approximate to 4-ply
1 hank fine black darning wool for eyes and markings
Crochet hooks Nos 7 and 9 (4·50 and 3·50 mm)
Stuffed shape

Method

FRONT

With cream wool and a No 9 (3·50-mm) hook, start at top of the face with 16 ch. Miss 1 ch, then work dc into following 15 ch.

Do 13 rows. Change to No 7 (4·50 mm) hook.

Next row: 3 ch to turn *, miss 1 st, 2 tr into next st, rep from * to end of row, finish with 1 tr. Rep 11 times. Break off wool.

BACK

With brown wool and a No 9 (3·50-mm) hook, make 24 ch.

Row 1: Miss 1 ch, then 23 dc.

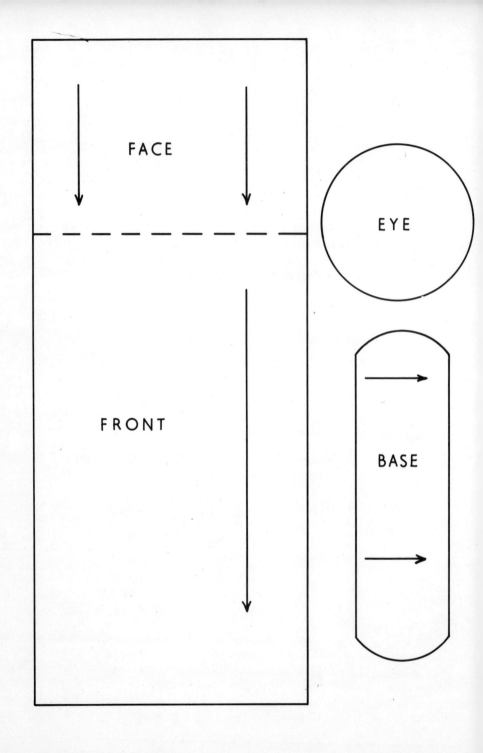

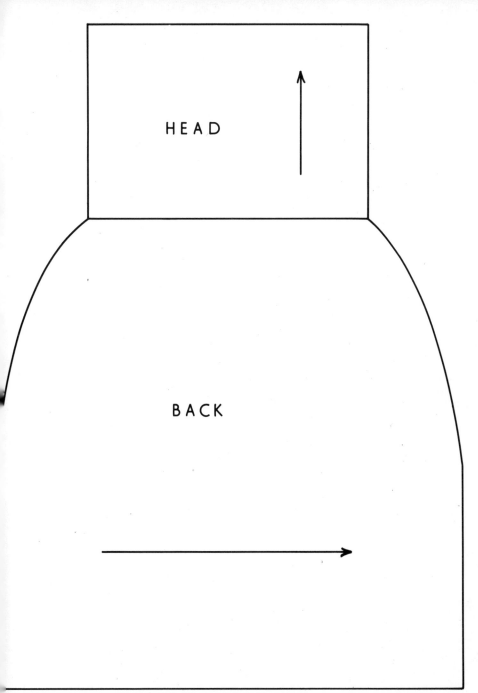

HEAD

BACK

Fig 14   Full-size pattern for owl

Row 2: 23 dc.

Row 3: 20 dc, turn.

Row 4: 20 dc.

Row 5: 23 dc. Rep rows 3 and 4. Then work 24 rows in dc. Rep rows 3, 4 and 5. Then work 2 rows in dc. Break off.

Join wool to narrow end of work and make 20 dc across top. Work 13 rows. Break off.

Pin these two pieces together over the stuffed shape and join with dc in brown wool, working on right side from bottom to top. Work 3 rows dc across top, decreasing 1 st in middle of each row to make dent over forehead. Then work dc from top to bottom down other side.

BASE

Make base with 14 ch; dc for 8 rows, increasing to 16 sts at 4th row, then decreasing again to 14 sts. Sew on base.

EYES

Make two flat circles in black wool, $1\frac{1}{4}$-in (3-cm) diameter, using No 9 (3·50-mm) hook in dc. Sew on to face. Using cream wool, embroider a bar-tack across centre of eyes about $\frac{1}{4}$ in (1 cm) wide.

With black wool, in chain stitch, embroider a line down the centre between the eyes, beak and feet.

The pussycat

This is made in stripes of two colours with contrasting colour for eyes. Nose and whiskers are embroidered in black. Crêpe wool originally used was purple and grey with lurex; eyes of green, but any variety of colours may be used. In fact, multi-coloured stripes would be amusing provided front and back are made to match. You can have fun with this one!

You will need

Small amounts of wool equivalent to 4-ply
Black wool or stranded cotton for embroidery
Hooks Nos 9 and 11 (3·50 and 3·00 mm)
Stuffed shape

Method

Stripes and base are worked in half trebles.
Head, eyes and ears in double crochet.

FRONT AND BACK

Using No 9 (3·50 mm) hook, make 23 ch.

Row 1: Miss 2 ch, 21 htr. 2 ch to turn on every row.

Row 2: 21 htr. Change to second colour.

Continue for 16 rows, changing colour every 2nd row.

Continue in stripes, shaping for neck and shoulders as follows:

Dec 1 st at each end of every row until 22 rows are worked, making 15 sts.

Row 23: Dec 1 st at each end.

Working in 1 colour and in dc, complete head: 3 rows dc.

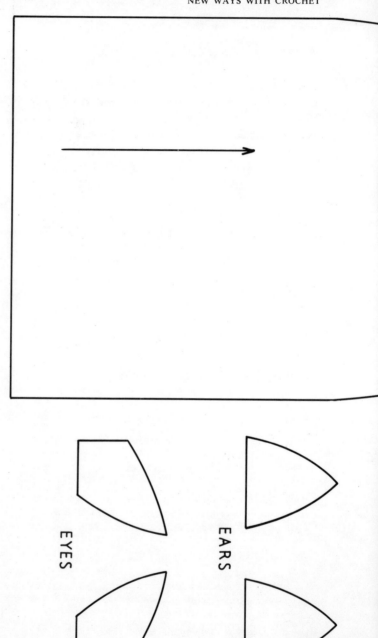

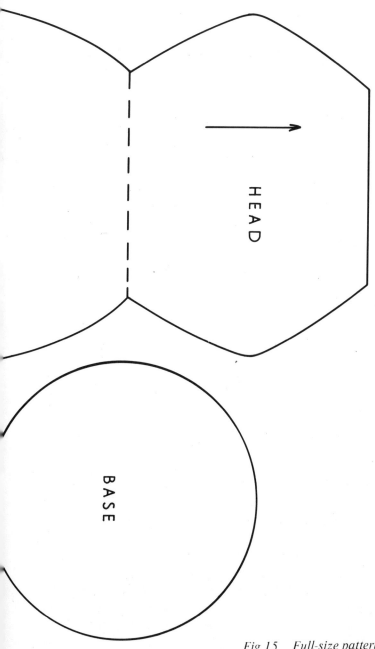

Fig 15   Full-size pattern for pussycat

Row 4: Inc 1 st at each end.

Row 5: Dc. Rep these two rows until 9th row.

Rows 9 and 10: Dc.

Rows 11, 12 and 13: Dec 1 st at each end.

Row 14: Dc.

Make two. Then join back and front together neatly, matching stripes and leaving base open. Stretch over stuffed shape.

TAIL

Make this by plaiting 30 strands of wool, approximately 8 in (22 cm) long. Bind one end into a tassel. Sew tail firmly to lining, bearing in mind its use as a handle.

BASE

Make circular base in htrs, using No 11 (3·00 mm) hook, completing each round as shown on page 20, until 3-in (7-cm) diameter. Sew to bottom of cat.

EARS

Using No 11 hook, make 7 ch. Work in dc for 7 rows, decreasing to fit pattern until 1 dc remains. Make 4, sew together in pairs and sew to corners of head, leaving a space of 5 dcs between. Starting halfway up the head and with the same coloured wool, work a continuous line in dc up side of head, around ear, 5 dcs between ears, round second ear and down to same level at other side.

EYES

Make two, using No 11 hook. Start with 2 ch, into 2nd make 1 dc. Inc at each until there are 5 dc, dec at each end until 1 dc remains. This will be a diamond shape. Pin and sew to the face leaving $\frac{3}{4}$ in (2 cm) between corners of eyes. Embroider a black slit in the centre of each, a small black nose and three fine whiskers at each side of it.

A bean bag

Plate 19   A bean bag

Small children like playing with bean bags; they're softer and easier than a ball to catch. This one has arms and legs too, so his appendages are catchable as well as his body.

Avoiding joins, the crochet is worked in one piece, narrowing towards
the top of the head. It can be in one colour or striped as in the picture,
when very small amounts of wool can be used up.

You will need

About ½ oz 4-ply wool, or oddments, for stripes
Minute pieces of felt for eyes and nose
No 9 (3·50-mm) hook
Lengths of Rya or thick wool for arms and legs
Stuffed shape
Dried peas or beans

Method

LINING

Cut two pieces of lining with turnings from pattern, stitch across base
and each side. Half fill with beans or peas, then sew across top.

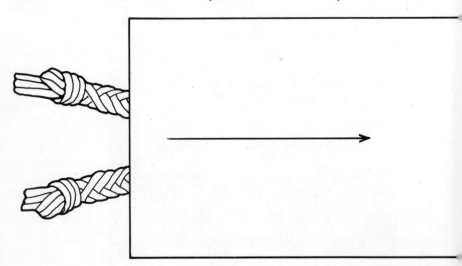

Fig 16   Full-size pattern for bean bag

THE CROCHET

Make 36 ch, join with ss into a circle. Work in dc for 34 rounds, completing each with a ss. If working in stripes, (which need not be of equal widths) join each colour carefully to avoid breaks in lines.

Now mark with cotton the beginning of the round and the 18th st. Continue in rounds, but decreasing 1 st above the marks in the next 9 rows, narrowing the head. Work 2 more rows dc, then join across top with 1 row dc. Slip over stuffed shape and sew across bottom.

TOPKNOT

Take 2 strands thick wool about 5 in (12 cm) long and knot through head, crochet *and* lining, at the centre.

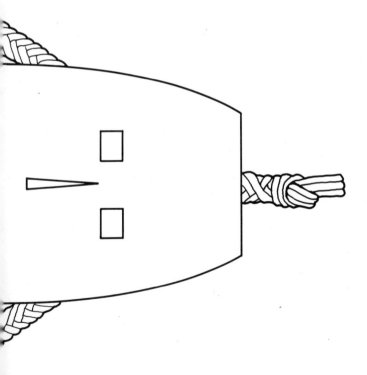

ARMS AND LEGS

Take 6 strands thick wool 12 in (30 cm), and push through crochet $\frac{3}{4}$ in (2 cm) below narrowing, using a wide-eyed needle. Arrange evenly, plait and knot ends. One at each side. Similarly, 6 strands, same length, twice, pushed through the base near the middle, will make the legs.

FACE

Cut two small squares of felt for eyes, sew to 'face' with one stitch through the middle.

Cut triangle for nose, sew long sides together and sew to face below eyes.

The frilly armadillo

The armadillo is a complicated creature with his sharp little burrowing
nose and shell-like armour and tail. Here he is made with a felt base,
ears and feet and eyes. He wouldn't fall into the category of a 'quickly
made' toy, if all these pieces were in crochet, though they could be.
(There's not really much that you can't do in crochet!) His most
interesting feature is his shell-stitch-covered body, but he is quite soft
and feels anything but armoured.

Plate 20   Armadillo

The first edition was made in Robin Tricel Perle which has a shiny
appearance and pleasing texture, but any 4-ply wool or yarn will do.
Colours can be what you will or what you have. These toys really
demonstrate the art of 'using-up' as they say in the cookery books.

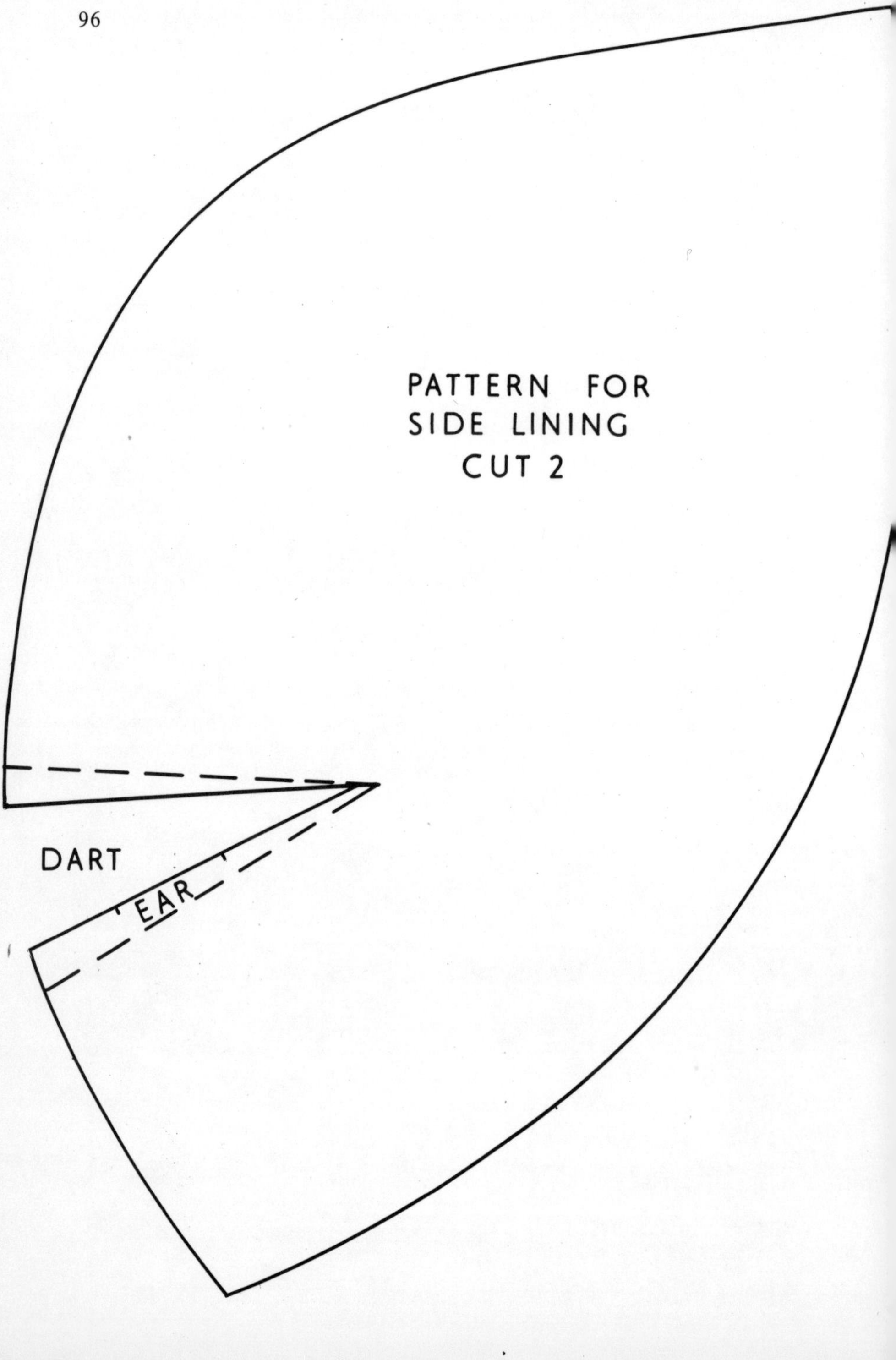

PATTERN FOR
SIDE LINING
CUT 2

DART

EAR

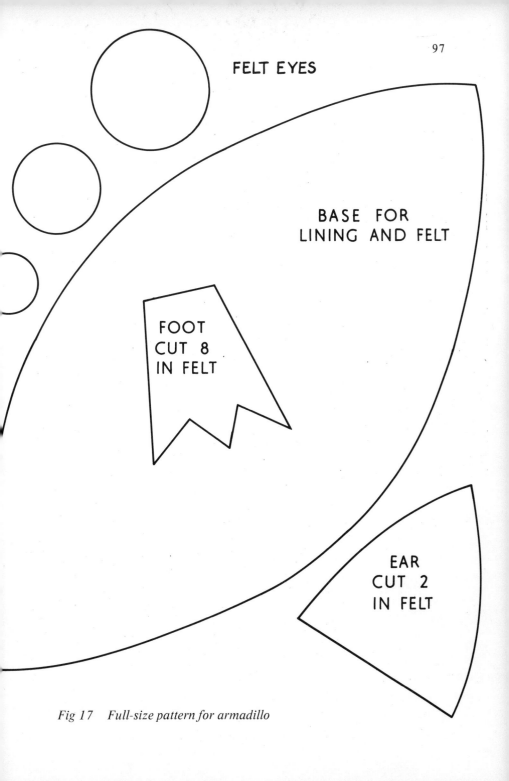

FELT EYES

BASE FOR
LINING AND FELT

FOOT
CUT 8
IN FELT

EAR
CUT 2
IN FELT

Fig 17   Full-size pattern for armadillo

You will need

1 oz main colour, 4-ply (suggested colour white)
1 oz second colour, for shells (suggested colour yellow)
1 square felt, 8 in (20 cm) (suggested colour green)
No 9 (3·50-mm) hook
Stuffed shape

Method

LINING

Cut all felt pieces and lining. Make a small pleat in each ear, and sew
them to the front of darts in lining. Then sew the darts and stitch the two
body pieces together along the top. Pin to the base and stitch, leaving 3
in (7·5 cm) open for stuffing. Stuff and sew up.

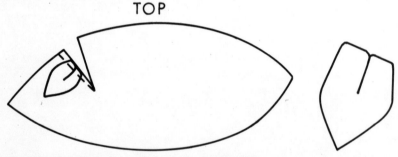

TOP

Fig 18   Method of attaching ears to armadillo

CROCHET THE NOSE FIRST

In main colour make 15 ch.

Work 14 dc for 12 rows.

Row 13: Dec 1 st at beginning of row.

Row 14: Dc.

Row 15: As row 13.

Row 16: Dc. Break off yarn. Make a second piece the same.

Sew these two pieces together at 'casting-on' edges.

The seam is the centre of the nose.

NOW MAKE THE BODY

This is made in a filet stitch of 1 tr, 1 ch, in two pieces. After these are joined together, the shells are worked into the filets.

Make 26 ch.

Row 1: 1 tr into 5th ch from hook. * 1 ch, miss 1 ch, 1 tr into next ch. Rep from * to end (12 sps). 4 ch, turn.

Row 2: Miss first tr. * 1 tr into next tr, 1 ch. Rep from *, ending with 1 tr into end ch sp. 4 ch, turn.

Row 3: Inc by working 1 tr into first tr, continue in pattern to end, 4 ch, turn.

Row 4: As 2nd (13 sps).

Row 5: As 3rd.

Row 6: As 2nd (14 sps).

Row 7: As 2nd.

Row 8: As 2nd, omitting 1 tr in ch sp at end of row.

Row 9: As 2nd.

Row 10: As 8th.

Row 11: As 2nd.

Row 12: As 8th.

Row 13: 1 tr in 3rd tr, continue in pattern.

Row 14: As 8th.

Row 15: As 13th, omitting 1 tr in last ch sp.

Row 16: 1 tr in 3rd tr. Continue in pattern.

Row 17: As 15th. Break off yarn.

Make a second piece. Sew these two together from the finishing point across the hump.

Starting at the 'casting-on' edge, and with the second colour, work a shell frill on every row, *across centre join*, breaking off at the end of each row. Finish at the tail end.

SHELL FRILL

Working on right side, attach yarn to first st.

Row 1: 5 tr in first ch sp, 1 dc in next ch sp. Rep to end. Break off.

Row 2: 1 dc in first ch sp, 5 tr in next. Rep. Break off.

THE TAIL

Make 34 ch in main colour. 1 tr into 5th ch from hook then work as for first row of body. In second colour make a shell frill from end to end.

Cut a triangle of felt $2\frac{1}{2}$ in (7·5 cm), 1 in (2·5 cm) at the top, tapering to a point. Sew into a tube. Starting at the point, sew the crochet in a spiral to the felt, making a stumpy tail.

MAKING UP

Pin centre front of frilled section to centre seam of lining; pin centre seam of nose piece to meet it and sew together between ears.

Join body and nose piece from ears to outside edge. Sew across front and back of ears to lining. Hem outside edge to lining at seam line and attach tail (firmly) to the end. Make four feet by joining together in pairs, stitching them together, then sew to lining at the points as shown in plate 20.

Make eyes from pattern, sewing smaller rounds in layers to the larger ones. Hem to sides of nose.

Pin on felt base and trim if necessary and hem all round.

Floppety Flo

Plate 21   Two dolls: Floppety Flo and Brown Betty

So long as dolls have two arms, two legs and some hair, they are
recognisable as such, even though they lack facial expression. This one
has simply two large spots on her face which might be either cheeks or

eyes, enough to make it a face. She's soft and sprawling and light in weight, suitable for the very young to hold or throw around. She is made *without* lining; the kapok filling is stuffed into the crochet shapes. Her legs and arms are striped in two colours and her dress is in felt to match one of them.

You will need

About $1\frac{1}{2}$ oz 4-ply wool or $\frac{3}{4}$ oz each of two colours
No 9 (3·50-mm) hook
2 squares felt, 8 in (20 cm)
Some Rya wool for hair

Method

ARMS

Make 30 ch. Work in dc (stripes of 2 rows of each colour, or plain), for 12 rows. Leave end for sewing up. Break off. Make two.

LEGS

Make 40 ch. Work as for arms. Make two.

BODY AND HEAD

This is worked in one piece and seamed up one side, so will be twice the shape of pattern.

Make 30 ch. Work 20 rows dc.

Row 21: Dec 1 st at each end and 2 sts in middle of row.

Row 22: Dc. Rep these two rows until reduced to 18 sts.

Then increase 1 st at each end and 2 sts in middle of each row, alternate rows dc, until 40 sts. Decrease as before in every other row, until there are 24 sts.

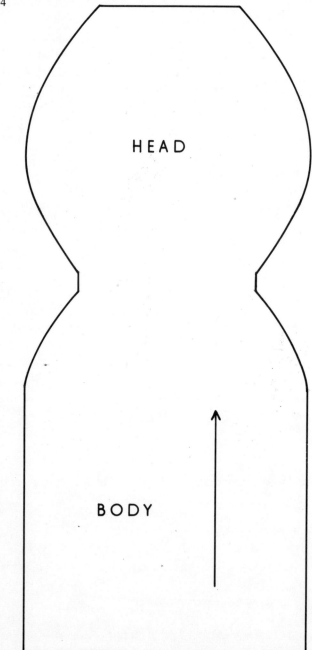

HEAD

BODY

Fig 19   Full-size pattern for Floppety Flo and Brown Betty

EG

ARM

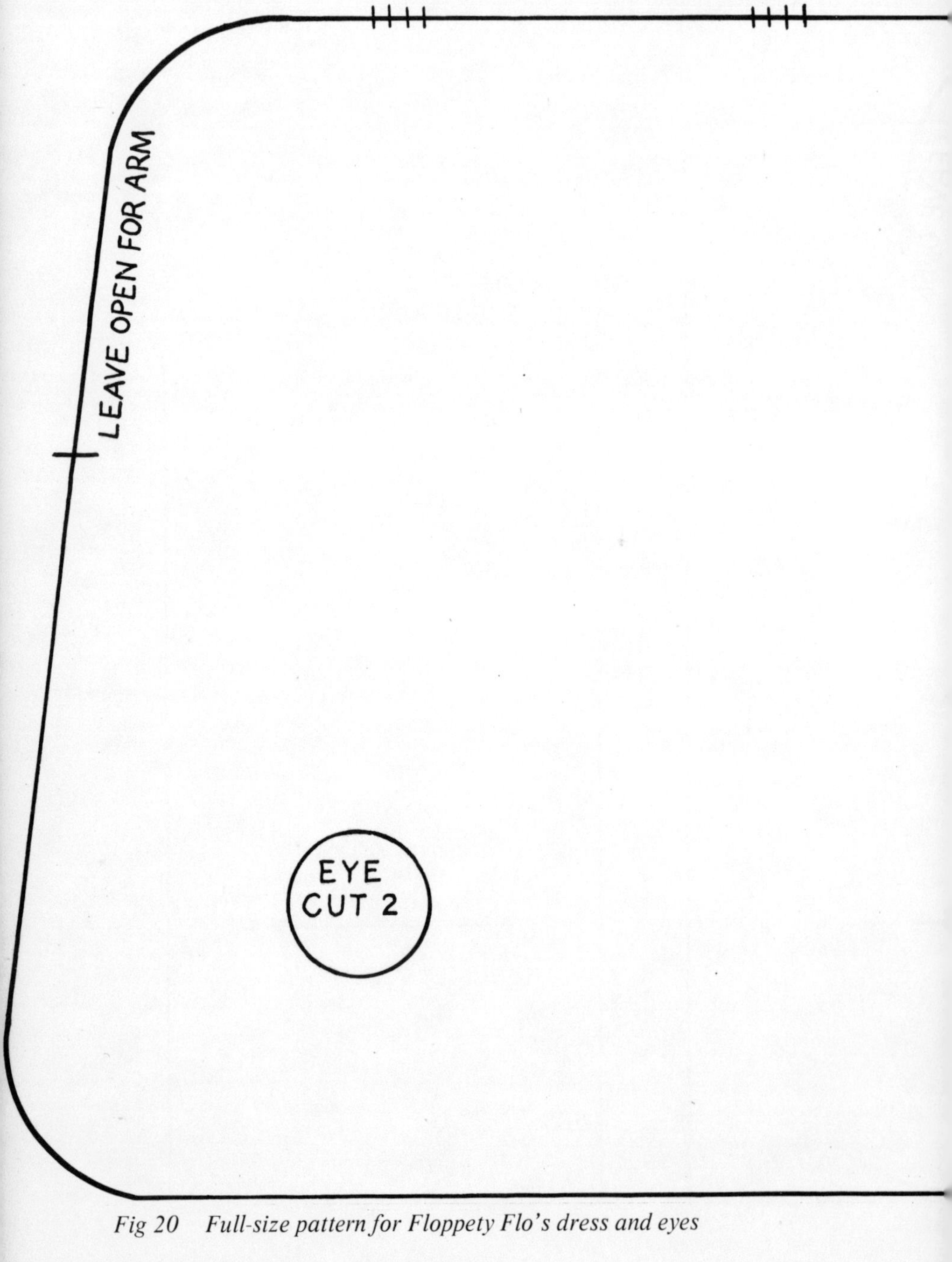

LEAVE OPEN FOR ARM

EYE
CUT 2

Fig 20   Full-size pattern for Floppety Flo's dress and eyes

LEAVE OPEN FOR ARM

MAKING UP

Sew across top of head and side seam, stuff with filling, sew across bottom. (If you like, two lollipop sticks firmly bound with adhesive can be inserted to stabilise neck and head. She's meant to be a floppy doll so this is really unnecessary.) Draw up short ends of arms and legs and sew up long sides. Stuff and sew up other end without drawing up. Sew these firmly to the body.

Take uneven lengths of Rya wool, or other thick wool, about 10 in (24 cm) long. Sew across top of head, making an untidy fringe at the front to hang over the face. Some of the long ends may be caught up in a little topknot, tied tightly with a piece of ribbon. A tidy head of hair is not the object of the exercise!

DRESS

Cut two pieces of felt for dress from pattern. Sew up sides, leaving opening for armholes as indicated on pattern. Join shoulders at points marked with dashes, *after* putting the dress on the doll, folding the material in at the neck. Sew two round patches on the face below the halfway mark.

Brown Betty

Because this doll is completely lined and because her legs appear to be a
little shorter, she has a more solid and less flighty appearance. Her hair
is curly, she wears a pretty dress and bangles and earrings, so is
altogether a more important person than Flo.

You will need

1 oz dark brown double knitting wool
1 oz black double crêpe wool, for hair (or finer wool used double)
No 7 (4·50-mm) hook
A piece of gay material, 18 by $7\frac{1}{2}$ in (45 by 18 cm)
Minute piece of white felt
9 brass rings, $\frac{3}{4}$ in (2 cm) in diameter
Stuffed shape in brown lining

Method

Make up lining from Floppety Flo's pattern, stuff firmly and sew up.
Keep arms and legs separate at present. Now make sections in double
crochet to fit the pattern, using the same method as for Flo and adapting
numbers of stitches because of larger hook and thicker wool.

Sew up as before and stretch over stuffed linings. Then join arms and
legs to body.

Make dress according to pattern and if material is soft, line it simply by
cutting two pieces, stitching together inside, making a tube, turning out
and finishing on right side. Actually, this is much easier than neatening
the whole thing in single material. Using black wool in a tapestry needle,
embroider loops all over head, using a thick pencil if necessary on
which to form the loops.

Sew two rings at ear position, give her one bangle and double anklet
rings. Cut two rounds white felt $\frac{1}{2}$ in (1·25 cm) and sew on to face below
the halfway mark.

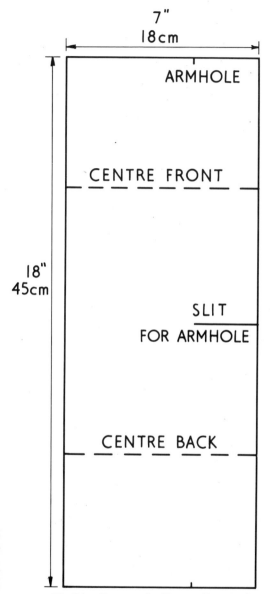

Fig 21   Pattern for Brown Betty's dress

5 No antimacassars, but some useful household things

We know that the fashion of yesterday is dowdy, the fashion of the day before absurd and the fashion of the day before that is charming. When I was young everything Victorian was regarded as laughable and tasteless; today Victoriana is in great demand. There is, at present, a reaction against the stark practicality of many of the household objects we use, especially those made of plastic, and a wave of nostalgia for the decorated exuberance of a hundred years ago. Scrubbed pine and homely kitchens are in and my own daughter refuses to have a laminated surface in hers. I being old-fashioned, have them in mine! I read recently that in the Seventies we might revert to crochet be-bobbled drapes on our mantel-pieces, so strong is this feeling for Victoriana. I cannot imagine that we would even want to revert to fireplaces, much less drapes. It is doubtful, too, if we shall ever return to that degree of refinement which demanded that a fish-paste jar should be clothed in a delicately crocheted container slotted and tied with blue ribbon round its neck, rather than have its label indecently exposed. Or that a jar containing jam should likewise have a crochet jacket with the word JAM cleverly incorporated in the design! We have become inured to jars and packets covered in advertising matter, even stamped unashamedly with prices in large print. What should we have to read if we covered them up? But forgoing some of the more horrible objects, such as hair tidies, piano-leg preservers and ostrich eggs encased in crochet mesh and hanging from gas brackets, so beloved by the Victorians, there are useful and decorative ways of using crochet around the house which will give the individuality so greatly desired by the young and fashionable.

Circular rug

Plate 22   Circular rug worked in bands of double crochet with scalloped insertions

This rug is worked in bands of double crochet with scalloped insertions at intervals. Though the original was made in one colour there are other possibilities, e.g. the bands might be worked in different shades of one colour, light shading to dark or vice versa. A brilliant effect could be obtained by using bright contrasting colours or two colours of the same yarn worked together would make it speckled—black and white, for instance. 'Health' cotton is available in colours besides white and used singly with a smaller hook would make a strong washable rug.

You will need

For a rug measuring 35 in (90 cm)
16 oz yarn, equivalent to double knitting and washable
No 5 (5·50-mm) hook
(If using health cotton, singly, 12 oz and No 6 hook)

Method

Yarn is used *double* throughout, each round is completed with a slip stitch and 1 chain to start next round. Bands are worked in double crochet.

Start with a ring of 4 ch.

1st round: 10 dc.

2nd round: Inc every other stitch.

3rd round: Inc every 3rd stitch.

4th round: Inc every 4th stitch.

5th round: Inc every 5th stitch.

6th round: Dc.

7th round: 1 dc, 3 ch, miss 1 dc. Rep.

8th round: 1 dc in dc of previous round, 3 dc over 3 ch, rep.

9th round: 1 dc, 2 ch, miss 3 dc, rep.

10th round: 3 dc over each 2 ch (missing the dc stitches). Rep.

The next band has 7 rows dc, followed by rounds, 7, 8, 9 and 10. The following band has 8 rows dc, then the scallops. And so on. Very little increasing is necessary in the plain bands as this is provided by the scallops.

When four bands have been worked, or whatever size of rug is required, finish with scalloped edge, rows, 7, 8, 9 and 10. Neaten off all ends, making rug reversible. Or mount on a piece of foam.

A bathmat

Take a piece of towelling in a suitable bright colour, decorate it with a panel of motifs and a border in thick white cotton, and you have a cheerful, washable bathmat. Any interesting motif will do—one is suggested here.

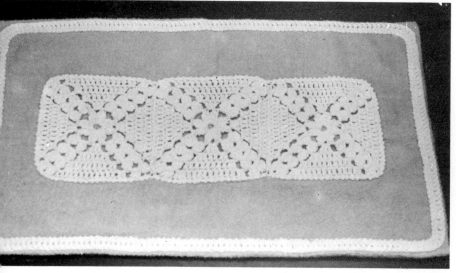

Plate 23   Bathmat decorated with crochet border and panel of motifs

You will need

Towelling in bathroom colour, 36 by 31 in (91 by 78 cm)
2 hanks white vest cotton
No 5 (5·50-mm) hook

Method

Fold material widthways and stitch edges together, leaving an opening to turn out. Turn, sew up opening making a rectangle of double material, 30 by 17 in (76 by 40 cm).

THE MOTIF

8 ch, join in a ring with ss.

Row 1: 3 ch (woh, hook into ring, draw through loop, woh, draw through 1 loop, woh, draw through 2 loops) twice, woh, draw through 3 loops, * 5 ch. Work from (to) 3 times, woh, draw through 4 loops, 2 ch. Work from (to) 3 times, woh, draw through 4 loops *. Rep from * to * 3 times, 2 ch, ss to 3rd ch of first 3 ch.

Row 2: 2 ss over 2 tr, 3 ch, work from (to) twice into 5 ch sp. Woh, draw through 3 loops, 2 ch. Rep from (to) 3 times into same ch sp. Woh, draw through 4 loops, 2 ch 3 tr into 2 ch sp, 2 ch. Continue working (1 gr, 2 ch, 1 gr) into 5 ch sp and (2 ch, 3 tr, 2 ch) into 2 ch sp to end of round. Join with ss into top of 3 ch.

Row 3: 1 ss, 3 ch * work (1 gr, 2 ch, 1 gr) into corner ch, 2 ch, 2 tr into 2 ch sp, 3 tr on 3 tr of previous row, 2 tr into 2 ch sp, 2 ch *. Rep from * to *, join with ss.

Rows 4 and 5: Work as last row, making trs on trs of previous row with 2 tr on either side in 2 ch sp. Join with ss.

Make two more motifs and join into a long panel.

Now work a corded edge all round. Press into shape, lay on the centre of towelling, sew at centres of motifs, through the two joins, and all round, sewing through the double material.

THE BRAID

Make a length of chain, approximately 270. Work 1 row trs, then on the 'casting-on' edge, work 1 row of corded edging. Lay braid evenly, leaving a $\frac{1}{2}$-in (1-cm) border of towelling, corded edge towards the centre. Sew both outer and inner edges of braid through double material.

One-square Afghan cushion

Frequently requested, this is the Afghan extended to 20 rows producing a cushion square of 16 in (40 cm). By using wools of different textures but the same thickness, interesting effects can be achieved. Colours can be a riot if using up, or a carefully balanced scheme. Obviously the outer rounds will require greater amounts of wool than the inner, which must be taken into consideration when planning the square.

Plate 24   One-square Afghan cushion

The pattern is a more open variation of the motif shown in Chapter 3 and takes approximately 4 oz double knitting thickness. No 7 (4·50-mm) hook.

Method

The 3 ch at the beginning of each round count as 1 tr.

MOTIF

6 ch, join in a ring.

Round 1: (3 ch 2 tr = 3 tr). 3 tr, 2 ch in ring, 4 times. Ss to top of 3 ch.

Round 2: ss to 2 ch sp (3 tr, 2 ch, 3 tr) in sp, 1 ch. * (3 tr, 2 ch, 3 tr) in sp, 1 ch. Rep from * twice. Ss to first st. Break off.

Round 3: Join new wool to 2 ch sp (hold end of old wool behind stitches and work over it). (3 tr, 2 ch, 3 tr) in sp, 1 ch 3 tr in 1 ch sp, 1 ch. * (3 tr, 2 ch, 3 tr) in 2 ch sp, 1 ch, 3 tr in 1 ch sp, 1 ch. Rep from * twice. Ss to first st. Break off.

Continue in this way, increasing the number of groups of 3 tr 1 ch between corners. Arrange colours as liked; bands of two or three rows of one colour are more effective than single rows but this depends on taste and what you have.

Back the cushion with furnishing fabric or make it two-sided if you have a lot of wool and time.

Round cushion

This again depends on colour for charm. Can be made in Crinkle-spun in three broad bands, 1 oz pale for centre, 2 oz darker and 3 oz darkest; or in left-over balls of wool in any colours. Use No 9 (3·50-mm) hook, or one appropriate to thickness of wools used.

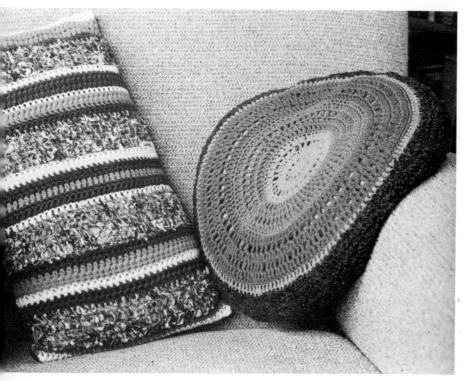

Plate 25   Two examples of crochet-covered cushions

Method

Make 4 ch, join in a ring. 14 tr, join.

Round 1: 3 ch, * 1 tr, 1 ch, rep from * to end. Join.

Round 2: 3 ch, * 3 tr under ch of previous round. Rep from *. Join.

Round 3: 3 ch, * miss 1 tr, (1 tr, 1 ch) into next, (1 tr, 1 ch) into next.
Rep from *. Join.

Round 4: 3 ch, * 2 tr under ch. Rep from * to end. Join.

Round 5: 3 ch, * miss 1, 1 tr, 1 ch, miss 1, (1 tr, 1 ch) into next, 1 tr into
next, 1 ch. Rep from *. Join.

Round 6: 3 ch, * 2 tr under each ch. Rep from *. Join.

Continue in rounds (see page 20) in trebles, interspersed with a round of
Round 3 for increasing, every three or four rounds. Work until the
required size is reached, then either make a second side or back this side
with material.

The round cushion illustrated is 16-in (40-cm) diameter.

Striped oblong cushion

Striking to look at, simple to make. All depends on the colours and variety of wools and the unevenness of the stripes. Strong bands of white next to dark colours are effective and the strong bands should be worked in double crochet to give solidity. Otherwise, rows of different stitches, trebles and half trebles, appropriate to the wools used, add interest. Bernard Klein's speckly mixtures were charming for this sort of thing, unfortunately no longer made, but the same effect is possible, mixing two strands of different colours.

The cushion illustrated was made in bright shades of green, orange, rust, dark brown, white, and a green and white mixture.

It measures 17 by 10 in (45 by 25 cm). Mostly double knitting wool, some of it crêpe, some of it finer and worked in an open treble. So it's a do-it-yourself cushion, depending on what you have in stock and what you want.

If you *have* to buy wool, then it must be 1 oz of each colour from which you'd probably have enough to make another, but planning it from what you have is fun.

Using a No 7 (4·50-mm) hook, make 80 ch. Work in variegated, uneven stripes in different stitches for about 17 in (45 cm). Don't press, join up long side, make a pad and finish off.

Place mats for the dining table

The country look

Made in natural-coloured cotton, these mats are thick and heat-proof. They will wash and wear for a lifetime, or until you tire of them. Although they conform to the 'scrubbed-pine-look' of today, they are equally effective on any wood, light or dark. The cotton can be had in colours, too, if preferred, but the natural colour has a distinguished charm.

Plate 26   Table mats—the country look

For six large mats and two smaller you will need:

5 four-ounce hanks Strutt's Dishcloth Cotton in natural
No 6 (5·00-mm) hook.

Crochet loosely 35 ch.

Row 1: * Miss 1 ch, (1 dc, 1 tr) in next ch. Rep from *.

Row 2 and every following row: 1 ch for turning, then (1 dc, 1 tr) into each dc of previous row. (17 patterns.)

Work 36 rows, inclusive, when mat will be $13\frac{1}{2}$ in (33·5 cm).

Make a fringe on the two short ends of mat by cutting cotton into $3\frac{1}{2}$-in (9-cm) lengths. Using hook and two strands together, draw through every other stitch and knot evenly. Press lightly, then trim fringe with scissors.

For small mats for vegetable dishes, make 25 ch and work as above (12 patterns). Work for 12 or 14 rows, then add fringe.

Ribbed mat

One 2-oz ball of Twilley's Knitcot will make one mat. As this is obtainable in a large range of colours, you may like to make a harlequin set, each mat a different colour, or alternate mats of two complementary colours. To see the full range should provoke original ideas.

Using No 7 (4·50-mm) hook, make 17 ch.

Row 1: Miss first ch, 2 dc in next, 14 dc, 3 dc in last ch. 14 dc down other edge of ch (and working over starting end of ch, thus eliminating it), 2 dc in last ch, join to first dc with ss. *Turn work.*

Subsequent rows are worked into the back thread of dcs only

Row 2: 2 dc in top st, 2 dc in next st, 15 dc, 2 dc in each of next 3 dc, 15 dc, 2 dc in next st, 1 dc in top st, join with ss. *Turn.*

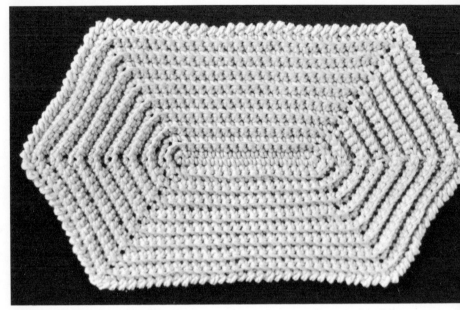

Plate 27   Ribbed table mat

Row 3: 2 dc in top st, 2 dc in next st, 16 dc, 2 dc in next st, 1 dc, 2 dc in top st, 1 dc, 2 dc in next st, 16 dc, 2 dc in next st, 1 dc, join to top st. *Turn.*

Row 4: 2 dc in top st, 2 dc, 2 dc in next st, 17 dc, 2 dc in next st, 2 dc, 2 dc in top st, 2 dc, 2 dc in next st, 17 dc, 2 dc in next st, 2 dc, join to top st. *Turn.*

Continue as in 4th row, increasing stitches between points in every row. Work 16 rows (8 ridges), then finish with a row of corded edging (see page 31).

6 Hats, caps and other wearable items

What we wear on our heads depends largely on hair fashions. In the last decade, with hair piled high, bouffant and beehive-like, with huge erections that might have done credit to an earlier Elizabethan age, hats have been almost an impossibility. It became fashionable to wear hair, instead.

Old films of the 1930s and 1940s, when doing without a hat hadn't been thought of, show hair worn high in front in a different manner, with hats like plates perched precariously on top. These make us laugh as no doubt the fashions in today's films will amuse our descendants.

So for many years there has been no room for the crochet expert with her warm little hats. She had her brief moment of glory after the last war when there was a demand for snoods, large crochet-net bags, worn over the long tresses that were popular. It was a short-lived fashion, possibly because there weren't many people who could make them.

Now with hair more sleek even though sometimes long and straggly, small hats are possible. In our fairly cold climate they are comfortable and necessary at certain times of the year. While the ski-ing cap has a stable design, there are fashion changes even in woolly hats; one year a beret with a bobble, the next a cap with a peak, then a quite close-fitting cap with a long scarf to match.

So long as you don't look as though you're wearing a tea-cosy, almost anything goes. Here is a variety of crochet head-gear that will help to see you through the vagaries of fashion. And some other things to wear.

Beret with variations

Make this in one hour—plus a little extra if you add a topknot.

Plate 28   Beret worked in a spiral

You will need

4 oz double knitting wool
Nos 5 and 7 (5·50- and 4·50-mm) hooks

Method

Using a plate measuring 10 in (26 cm) in diameter, cut a circle of thick paper.

Draw on it an inner ring, 5 in (12·5 cm), using a small plate or saucer. This is your pattern.

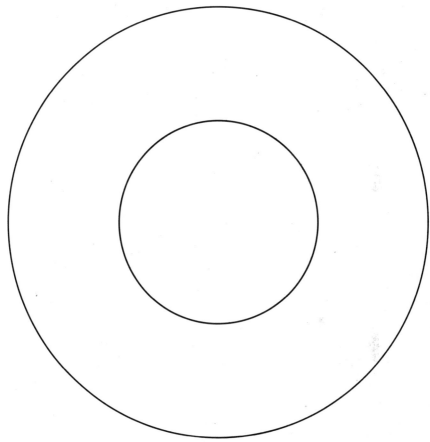

Fig 22   Beret pattern

Using two strands together and No. 5 hook, make 4 ch, join with ss. Work 12 tr into the ring. Then, 2 tr into each of the 12 tr.

Now, working in a spiral, i.e. *not* completing each round, continue in tr until the size of the pattern is reached, keeping the work flat with increases which get fewer as the circle gets larger. Mark the start of the next round with coloured cotton.

Round 1: Dec every 5th st.

Round 2: Tr.

Round 3: Dec every 4th st.

Round 4: Tr.

Round 5: Dec every 4th st.

This brings you to the size of the inner circle, and an average head size.

With No 7 (4·50-mm) hook and single wool work 2 dc into every st. Finally, 1 row dc. Finish off, add top decoration if liked.

Variations

1   Use two different-coloured double knitting wools to make a tweed effect.

2   Use 1 strand quick-knit wool and 1 of mohair for a fluffy beret.

3   Use 3 strands 4-ply wools in different colours.

4   Make beret smaller for a child, using a smaller paper pattern.

5   Finish the top with a knob, like a mushroom stalk, made as follows:

No 7 hook, 1 strand wool. 6 ch, 7 rows dc, sew up long side and top, stuff with oddments of matching wool or cotton wool. Sew firmly to centre.

6   Traditional finish of pompom in plain or mixed colours. Make it on two $2\frac{1}{2}$-in (6·5-cm) rings of cardboard, a smaller ring cut in the middle of each. Using wool in 3 or 4 strands, wind through centre hole and over edge until no more can be squeezed in. With pointed scissors cut wool between cardboard, tie firmly into middle, then remove cardboard.

7   Add a peak, as in 'Hat With Peak' to make a baker-boy beret.

8   Add a shaggy tassel. Use cardboard, 3 by 4 in (7·5 by 10 cm), and wind wool round 3-in side until thick. Tie wool round one fold several times, tightly. Cut other fold. Sew on.

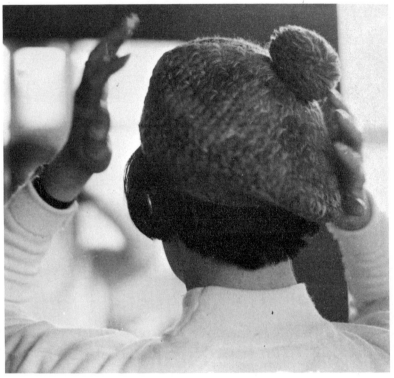

Plate 29   Beret made of mixture of two wools with pompom

Easily made ski cap

Plate 30   Ski cap and mittens worked in mixture of two wools
decorated with edelweiss flowers

This too, can be crocheted in an hour and has endless permutations. It can, for example, be made in stripes of three rows of different colours, or worked in a mixture of two wools used together, with plain edge and pompom. Mine was made in charcoal and white Paton's Bracken wool with white trimmings, but any interesting double knitting wool can be used.

You will need

2 oz double knitting wool
About $\frac{1}{2}$ oz contrast
No 7 (4·50-mm) hook

Method

The crochet is worked up and down the height of the head.

Make 27 ch (height of head, approx. 7 in or 17 cm).

Row 1: 1 tr into 3rd ch, 18 tr, 1 htr, 4 dc, 1 ss, turn.

Row 2: 1 ch, miss ss, 4 dc, 1 htr, 20 tr, turn.

Row 3: 2 ch, miss first tr, 19 tr, 1 htr, 4 dc, 1 ss, turn.

Repeat rows 2 and 3 until work measures 22 in (60 cm) measured at tr edge. Sew seam. With contrast, work 12 rows dc round lower edge. At upper edge, insert hook into every row and pull through a loop, break off wool and draw all loops together. Fasten off and attach pompom in contrast, to middle of cap.

And mittens to match

You will need

3 oz Patons Bracken double knitting wool, or similar tweedy mixture
1 oz contrast double knitting wool
Nos 7 and 9 (4·50- and 3·50-mm) hooks

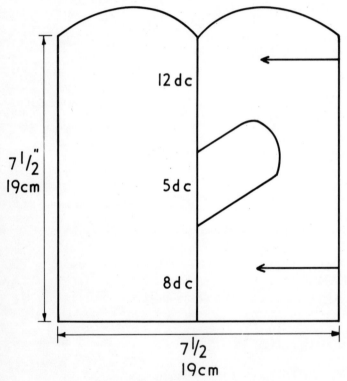

Fig 23   Pattern for mittens

Method

Cut a pattern for guide from diagram, enlarging or reducing in size.
This shape, for instance, makes useful mittens for a child. If size is
altered, adjust number of stitches to fit pattern. Work in dc throughout,
observing rule for turning at ends of rows.

LEFT-HAND MITT

Using No 7 hook, make 27 oh, work 2 rows dc. Continue for 14 rows altogether, increasing 1 st at beginning of 3rd, 5th and 7th rows, then decreasing at beginning of 9th, 11th and 13th rows.

15th Row: 12 dc, 9 ch. The thumb is worked on these sts.

THUMB

8 dc. Make 12 rows altogether, increasing at end of each row until there are 12 dc, then decreasing at each end until there are 8 dc. Break off wool, leaving an end of 1 yd. With this, sew across top of thumb, drawing in slightly, and the seam. Sew half the base of thumb to the next 5 dc of main row, then finish working to end or row in dc. Join on ball of wool.

16th row: Work up to base of thumb, make 7 dc across open edge. Continue to end. Inc 1 st.

Continue for 13 more rows, first increasing then decreasing to make shape correspond to front of mitten.

Break off wool, sew across top, drawing up slightly, sew seam. With contrast wool and No 9 hook, take up 30 sts at wrist. Work 12 rows dc, break off and finish.

RIGHT-HAND MITT

Make similarly, but after 16th row, turn thumb inside out and continue as before. This will reverse mitt for right hand.

An Edelweiss flower seems an appropriate decoration though it is optional. Make three, one for the hat, from instructions given on page 44.

Close-fitting cap in star stitch

Plate 31   Cap in star stitch

You will need

4 oz double knitting wool
No 5 (5·50-mm) hook

Two thicknesses of wool are used together for this hat which fits an
average-sized head.

Method

Using two strands of wool, make 69 ch, join in a ring.

Round 1: 2 ch, htrs to end of round, join with ss.

Round 2: *Star Stitch*   4 ch, hook into 2nd ch from hook, draw through loop, hook into 3rd ch, draw through loop, hook into 4th ch, draw through loop. Draw loops through each of the next 2 htrs (6 sts on hook), woh, draw through all loops, 1 ch to form eye. (1 star completed.)

* Hook into eye of previous star, draw through loop, hook into last loop of previous star, draw through loop, hook into last htr already worked into, draw through loop, hook into next 2 htrs, draw through loops (6 loops on hook), woh, draw through all loops, 1 ch to form eye (2nd star completed). Rep from * to end of round. Join last star to first with ss. Turn.

Round 3: Working on wrong side and in the opposite direction, make 2 ch. * 1 htr into eye of last star, 1 htr into top loop of last star, (2 sts in each star), rep from * to end. Join with ss, turn.

Rounds 2 and 3 form pattern. Rep, making 5 pattern rounds.

Round 12: Dec in each star by drawing loops through first and third htrs, thus decreasing 1 st in every star.

Round 13: htrs.

The remainder is worked in 1 strand only.

Round 14: As 12th.

Round 15: Htrs.

Round 16: As 12th.

Round 17: Htrs.

Break off wool, leaving long end to draw up centre sts, and to draw together any spaces in the back seam.

Hat with peak

This hat is worked in groups of double trebles; and double crochet worked in two thicknesses of wool to give firmness. It is finished with a peak and cord trimming.

Plate 32   Hat with peak worked in groups of double trebles and double crochet

You will need

4 oz double knitting wool
No 7 (4·50-mm) hook

Method

HAT

1 Using single wool, make 3 ch, join into ring. 4 ch.

2 15 dtr into ring (the 4 ch count as 1 dtr, making 16 altogether). Join with ss. 4 ch.

3 2 dtr into every st. Join with ss. 4 ch.

4 Groups. 4 dtr (4 ch count as first dtr) into next sp. Leave last loop of each on hook, woh, draw through all loops, making 1 gr. 1 ch, miss 1 sp. Rep, making 17 grs. Join. 4 ch.

5 * Make 1 gr into top of gr, 1 ch, 1 dtr into sp between grs, 1 ch, * rep. (18 grs.) Join. 4 ch.

6 * Make 1 gr into top of gr, 1 ch, 1 gr into dtr, * rep. Join. 4 ch. (35 grs).

7 Make 1 gr into top of gr, 1 dtr in sp between grs, rep. (35 grs). Join. 1 ch.

8 Now using *two* strands of wool, 1 dc into top of gr and into sp at each side of dtrs. Join 1 ch.

9 1 dc into every dc. Join, 1 ch.

10 * 6 dc, dec 1. * Rep. Join, 1 ch.

11 Dc into every st. Join, 1 ch.

12 As 10.

13 As 10. Join 4 ch.

14   With single wool, 1 gr into every other dc. Join. 1 ch.

15   With double wool, 1 dc into gr, 1 dc into sp between grs. Rep. Join 1 ch.

16   To give hat more height at the front, an extra row of dc is worked across front half only. Divide sts and using double wool, work 1 row dc on half of sts. Break off wool.

17   Continue in dc from position where extra row started. For 2 rows dec every 6th st.

19   Insert another extra half row, as in 16.

20   Dc. Join.

THE PEAK

Continue to work in dc across front half of hat, increasing at every 4th st in first row. Work 5 rows, decreasing at each end of each row to shape peak. Work 1 row dc all round hat and peak, break off end and sew in.

THE CORD TRIMMING

Take 12 lengths of wool at least 3 times as long as the length of cord required. Tie the ends together and fasten to a hook on the wall. Twist the opposite end round and round until very tight. Detach from the hook and let the two ends twist together to form a cord. Bind one end leaving fringe. Sew at one end of peak with buckle or ornament and attach at other end of peak.

Country hat with brim

Suitable for a gusty day, this is made in a lovat green mixture with a twisted cord trimming. Because the crown is fairly high, some stiffening is necessary and a piece of Vilene or other firm light-weight material may be used. Quite often a little stiffening of this sort gives shape to any crochet hat or cap and should be experimented with.

Plate 33   Country hat with twisted cord trimming. The crown is stiffened with Vilene

You will need

4 oz Paton's Flair treble knitting
Nos 5 and 7 (5·50- and 4·50-mm) hooks
Piece of stiffening, approx $4\frac{1}{2}$ by 23 in (11·5 by 59 cm)
Petersham ribbon to match

Method

Using No 5 hook, make a ring of 4 ch.

Round 1: 8 dc into ring (1 ch 1 dc = 1 patt.).

Round 2: 1 ch 1 dc in every dc. Join. (8 patts.)

Round 3: Work 2 patts in each ch. Join. (16 patts.)

Round 4: Inc 1 patt in every other ch. Join. (24 patts.)

Round 5: Work 1 patt in every ch. Join—and at end of each round.

Round 6: Inc 1 patt in every 3rd ch (32).

Rounds 7 and 8: As round 5.

Round 9: Inc 1 patt in every 4th ch (40).

Round 10: As round 5.

Round 11: Inc 1 patt in every 5th ch (48).

Rounds 12–23: As round 5.

Round 24: Make 4 decreases, 1 every 10 patts.

Rounds 25–33: Dc in every stitch, using No 7 hook.

BRIM

Work in double yarn, No 5 hook.

Round 1: Dc, inc in every 5th st.

Rounds 2, 3 and 4: Dc in every dc.

Round 5: Turn work and make 1 row corded edging on under side of brim.

Cut a piece of stiffening 4 in (10 cm) deep and your head measurement plus turnings. Join in a ring and make a $\frac{1}{2}$-in (1·25-cm) turning on one edge. Pin the single edge inside hat above brim-line, drawing in the crochet to size if necessary. Catch stitch to crochet. Neaten join with a band of petersham ribbon.

A twisted cord, about 27 in (70 cm) and with tasselled ends can be used as trimming if liked (see page 45).

Shaggy-topped helmet

Plate 34   Helmet with ear-piece worked in mohair and ordinary wool

Winter weather hat with ear-pieces, tying under chin, cosy for a child
and sensible for a grown-up, too. Make it in Robin 'Shaggy Darling', or
using one strand mohair with one strand double knitting, and double
knitting for the lower part.

You will need

1 oz 'Shaggy Darling' and 1 oz double knitting *Or* 1 ball mohair and 2 oz double knitting
Nos 5 and 7 (5·50- and 4·50-mm) hooks

Method

Using No 5 hook and working in trs, make the crown in mohair, keeping the shape flat until 9 in (22·5 cm) in diameter.

Continue in trs, decreasing every 6th tr for 3 more rows. You will now have used up the mohair wool, and have approx 62 sts. Change to double knitting and No 7 hook and work the remainder of the hat backwards and forwards, finishing each row at centre back with ss, and turning with 1 ch. Work 6 rows dc.

Mark centre front and count 10 sts to either side of it, mark with cotton.

Next row: work to first mark, turn, work round to 2nd mark, turn, work to centre back.

For ear-pieces, mark 13 sts to either side of centre front. Work from back to first mark, turn and work across 13 sts, turn. Work 10 rows on these sts, decreasing 1 st at the end of each row until 4 sts remain.

Break off wool.

Work second ear-piece, then 1 dc all round hat.

Continue working on the 4 sts of ear-piece for 50 rows to make tying strap.

Work strap on second ear-piece, slightly longer.

Striped bag and belt

Plate 35   Striped bag and matching belt worked in double crochet

Make these to wear with summer dresses appropriate to your general
colour scheme. Use either thick cotton or any of the man-made yarns
which give an attractive fabric when worked. The original was made in
stripes of black, purple and bright pink, but one can imagine an orange,
yellow, black sequence, or indeed any colour combination.

Although instructions are given for a bag measuring 10 by 5 in (25·5
by 12·5 cm), when finished, and made in the equivalent of double
knitting wool, the pattern is a simple rectangle and to make a different
size merely involves cutting a pattern of the size required and measuring
the numbers of stitches and rows necessary to fit it.

The simple dc stitch takes on a new interest when worked in coloured
stripes.

You will need (for bag and belt)

1 oz or ball of each chosen colour
No 7 (4·50-mm) hook
Piece of felt for lining 9 by 14 in (22·5 by 35 cm)
Piece of buckram or cardboard, 9 by 5 in (22·5 by 12·5 cm)
2 in Velcro for fastening
Buckle, 2 in inside measurement

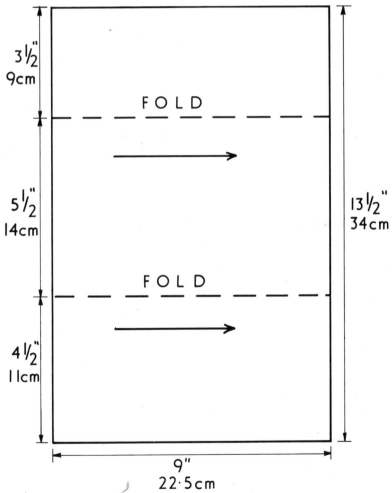

Fig 24   Pattern for striped bag

Method

BAG

Work entirely in dc. Make 60 ch. Work 3 rows in main colour, then 2
rows of each other colour alternately. Finish with 3 rows main colour.
Across one end, work 3 rows main colour to complete border of flap.
Neaten other end of crochet by joining to felt and forming a narrow felt
binding. Fold felt $4\frac{1}{2}$ in (11·5 cm) from binding, sew down each end.
Fold crochet 5 in from binding and sew down each end. Tuck felt 'bag'
into crochet 'bag', then insert stiffening between felt and crochet. Trim
felt to meet inner edge of flap border and hem to it. Cut two pieces
Velcro, sew to felt at each end of flap and at corresponding position on
bag.

BELT

Make a loose ch in the darkest colour, equal to your waist size plus 5 in
(12·5 cm). Work 12 rows dc, 2 rows of each colour. Mitre one end,
increasing 1 st every other row from 1st to 6th row, then decreasing
from 6th to 12th row, similarly. Cover buckle in crochet as described
on page 41, if liked, and sew on.

Stiffening is not really necessary, but, if required, 2-in (5-cm) adhesive
tape should be pressed on the wrong side.

Ring belt

Plate 36   Belt made of crochet-covered rings

If you are a purist you will probably prefer a belt made from the same material as a dress, particularly if the dress is in crochet. This one is made from rings covered with crochet and any wool or yarn may be used for it. Lurex mixture would make a decorative belt for any plain dress.

Obviously any size of ring can be covered and more rings of a smaller size and less of a larger will be needed. It is difficult therefore to stipulate numbers and amounts of wool, but 1 oz will usually cover enough rings for a belt.

For a normal waistline, buy 36 metal or plastic rings, approx 1 in (2·5 cm) in diameter. Tie on wool and with hook appropriate to wool, work in dc all round until firmly covered, putting the hook inside the ring and drawing the wool through for each stitch. Work over the short end of wool, too, to neaten. Join with ss, then continue without breaking off on a second ring. Cover the rings, in pairs in this way, then sew the pairs together. A small hook and embroidered loop may be sewn on two rings in appropriate place to fasten, or the belt may be tied loosely.

Layabout socks

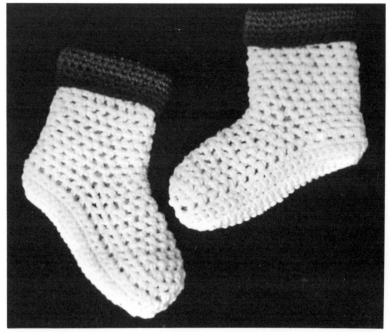

Plate 37   Child's socks for lounging around the house

Warm and comfortable for playing around the house and will fit a child
of seven to ten years. Made in a dark colour with a light 'cuff' probably
most sensible, though the original cream with shaded orange cuff looks
attractive.

You will need

3 oz any 4-ply wool, used double
Oddments of contrast 4-ply wool for cuffs
No 5 (5·50-mm) hook

Method

Each sock takes $1\frac{1}{2}$ oz wool, so divide one ball into two.

Using two strands together, make 38 ch.

Row 1: Miss 3 ch, * 1 htr in next ch, 1 ch, miss 1 ch. Rep from * ending with 1 htr in last ch. (18 htr.)

Row 2: 2 ch, * 1 htr in first space, 1 ch, miss 1 htr. Rep from * ending with 1 htr in last chain.

Repeat 2nd row throughout.

Work 8 more rows. Don't break off wool.

With new wool, work over the 8 middle htr in pattern (2 ch, 7 htr) for 11 rows to make the top of the foot. Break off wool.

Continuing from the edge, with original wool, work round to the other edge. (39 htr.)

Turn and work another row. In the next two rows, dec 1 htr at the centre of foot. (To decrease, after 1 ch, woh, draw loop through next sp. Hook into following sp, woh, draw through 4 loops on hook.)

Work now in dc, making 1 dc in first sp, 2 dc in next sp. Rep to end.

Work 3 more rows in dc, decreasing 1 stitch at the end of each row, and 1 stitch in the middle of last row. Sew up foot and back seam.

THE CUFF

Work on wrong side and with double contrast wool. Pick up 32 stitches round the top and work 10 rows in dc. Fasten off. A striped effect, using oddments of different colours is pretty.

Crochet-edged poncho

Plate 38   Crochet-edged poncho

This garment of South American origin is popular now in many other
parts of the world, especially in the colder climates. The Finns have
adopted it and make it in their fine woollen materials and the striking
colours for which they are renowned. It tops trousers very elegantly and
apart from giving one a feeling of gaiety—an attribute one could never
apply to our national body-warmer, the cardigan—it is warm and
comfortable, leaving the hands and arms unhampered for chores and
perhaps crochet. Made entirely in crochet it is rather heavy. I
compromised with a square of material, crochet-edged and fringed.
The material should be warm, and can be wool, printed, striped or plain,
even fine tweed, velvet, corduroy or any of the man-made winter-weight

cloths. If you have a piece in stock, left over from dressmaking, a square 32 in is the approximate size required. If you have to buy—

You will need

1 yard 36-in material, from which you will get a straight collar.
Or $\frac{7}{8}$ yard 54-in material, from which you will get a cross-way collar.
(If you use up an oddment, you can make a crochet collar.)
Wool, minimum 6 oz 4-ply, but depending on depth of edging and fringe. Can be one colour or several, depending on material.
No 9 (3·50-mm) hook.

Method

Cut material 32 in square. Turn in a narrow hem and finish by hand, *or* turn up with cross-way binding to tone with material. With wool and crewel needle, embroider chain stitch all round. Now, starting in the middle of one side, make 1 row treble, allowing 3 treble in each corner chain.

Subsequent rows can be in any chosen stitch, but care must be taken to make symmetrical corners.

Make the last row with chain spaces, e.g. 2 tr, 2 ch, which will allow room for tassels.

For tassel, cut 6 5-in lengths of wool, fold in half, push fold through space from front to back, draw ends through fold and pull tightly.

NECKLINE

Fold poncho diagonally and again in half to find centre. Mark. Cut through diagonal fold 5 in (12·5 cm) either side of centre mark, making a 10-in (25·5-cm) slit. Scoop out neckline to 1-in (2·5-cm) depth at centre back and front. Make straight collar by joining the two pieces cut from 36-in material, 23 in (60 cm) long, joined in a circle. Pin on, seams to ends of slit, stitch and hem.
Or if 54-in material was used, cut cross-way collar, 9 in wide (22·5 cm), 23 in (60 cm) long, join in circle and attach similarly

Or if no material available, bind edges of neck, chain stitch all round, and crochet double band to correspond with edging.

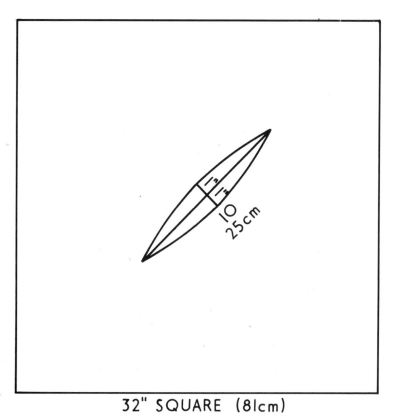

32" SQUARE (81cm)

Fig 25   Method of making neck-opening in poncho

An alternative one-colour edging

If you want to use less wool, this lacy openwork border is the answer. Using jersey material for the poncho, turn up single hem, $\frac{1}{4}$ in (1 cm) and herring-bone all round.

Plate 39   Detail of poncho edging

You will need

4 oz 4-ply wool
No 9 (3·50-mm) hook

Method

Work chain stitch on the edge, using a crewel needle and wool.

Now make 1 row dc. (Increase appropriately at corners.)

2nd row: 1 htr 2 ch, miss 1 sp, rep.

3rd row: 1 htr on 1 htr, 5 ch, 1 htr into same stitch, 5 ch, miss 1 htr, rep.

4th row: 1 htr into the 3rd ch of the ch st between the 2 htrs worked into 1 stitch of previous row, 3 ch, 1 htr, 3 ch 1 htr into the same stitch, 3 ch 1 dc into the 3rd ch of the next 5 ch, 3 ch, rep.

FRINGE

Using a piece of cardboard, cut 4 6-in (15-cm) lengths of wool for each tassel. Several lengths may be cut at a time. With a large crochet hook pull the four strands through each of the two small scallops at the deepest part of the border and knot. Split each tassel and knot half of one to half of the next. Press lightly, then trim edges of the fringe with scissors.

An all-crochet poncho in three colours

This is made from four rectangles joined together as in diagram. An edging in two colours surrounds the square thus made, finished with a fringe. Children like wearing these attractive creations and this method is easily adapted for a smaller wearer, simply by making the initial rectangles less in size.

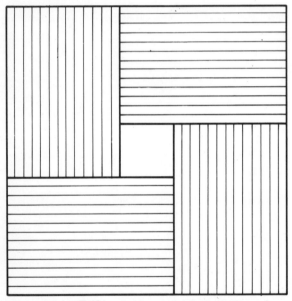

Fig 26   Arrangement of squares for an all-crochet poncho

Each rectangle is 15 by 9½ in (30 by 24 cm).

Overall size without fringe is 30-in (78-cm) square.

You will need

8 oz double knitting, double crêpe or Pingouin Crylor
4 oz in lighter shade

4 oz in contrasting colour
No 5 (5·50-mm) hook

Method

Make 45 ch, work 43 htrs, turn each row with 2 ch, continue until work measures $9\frac{1}{2}$ in (24 cm). Make three more rectangles. Join carefully as in diagram. With lighter shade work 4 rows in htrs all round, 4 htrs at each corner.

With contrast work 7 rows similarly.

Cut 9-in (22·5-cm) lengths of lighter wool, and using 3 strands together knot tassels round outer edge at every 4th stitch.

With dark wool, work 1 row dc all round neck opening.

7 Making clothes–a fresh approach

Although crochet stitches are generally worked horizontally across a garment there is no reason why they should not be worked vertically. The two main attributes of crochet—it keeps its shape and wears endlessly—apply, whichever way it is used. Worked vertically, the lines of pattern run downwards, often an advantage to the wearer. We all know that horizontal lines don't make people look thinner and plump figures tend to look plumper in most crochet clothes because of this. A simple example of this vertical method is shown in the child's skirt on page 178.

So far as children are concerned, crochet, as the Duchess remarked in another circumstance, is much too good for them—it lasts too long! The obvious answer is to start at the top and work downwards. Then you can add on as the child grows. And for a reverse reason if clothes for a teenager are worked from the top, you can always wind off a few rows at the hem to achieve the 'mini-extent' required. Or wind off still further rows to turn a dress into a tunic to wear with pants.

We all fondly hope to look like the elegant model on the cover of a pattern, though this is a rare result. So many of us have figure peculiarities that it would be an impossibility for pattern designers to cater for all our variations. So it would seem sensible to plan a garment from a pattern that fits, and assuming that most craftswomen have a nodding acquaintance with dressmaking, it is possible to combine that knowledge with crochet to produce clothes which are well-fitting and original.

Quite simply, if you have a favourite pattern which always succeeds (I have a tattered blouse pattern from which everything from a nightie to a topcoat—and many crochet clothes too—have been made) all you have to do is to adapt it for crochet. Eliminate the turnings, pin up any darts—crochet will mould conveniently over curves—decide on lengths required and make allowances for any borders which may be added.

Having marked such alterations on the pattern, cut a new whole one
which will be the shape of your crochet garment. Work out the number
of stitches required according to the thickness of wool, the size of hook,
and your tension. This will involve a little trial-and-error operation at
the start, necessary for any pattern. Then, too, any stitch or
combination of stitches can be used, an advantage in these days when to
be original is to be fashionable.

Another point. Why must we always have side seams? Some stitches
create an uneven edge, difficult to join in a neat seam, e.g. star stitch
which has scalloped edges. In this case, and indeed generally, it is
possible to omit side seams altogether and to work from front edge
across back and to other front edge, all in one. When armhole level is
reached you find that you've almost finished the garment, surprisingly
quickly. If you are pear-shaped, then the bottom of a jacket or cardigan
must be wider than at the bust, in which case, some decreasing at the
under-arm is necessary and possible.

Sun-suit for doll

Plate 40   Sun-suit for doll which can easily be adapted for a child .

To take a simple example, let us make a sun-suit, jacket and pants, for a doll 16 in (40·5 cm) high. Front and back patterns are shown here and can be copied easily for a larger or smaller doll.

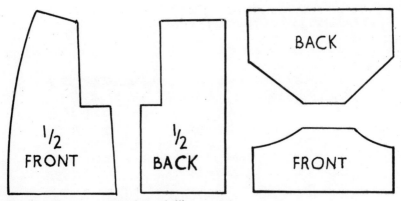

Fig 27   Pattern pieces for a doll's sun-suit

It is obviously unnecessary to crochet these small sections separately, and by putting the side seams of the jacket together and the crutch join of the pants, the outfit can be made in just two pieces instead of five, avoiding seams and saving time. Measurements, in this case, are given in centimetres.

Method

Draw fronts and back pattern, full size and in one piece. Draw pants pattern in full size, joining at crutch. Cut out, and the pattern is ready to follow in crochet. Work in dc throughout, following the shape of the patterns. Use 1 oz white, 1 oz brightly coloured DK wool. No 7 (4·50-mm) hook.

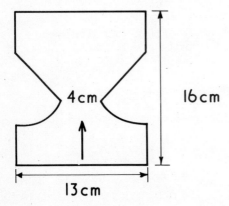

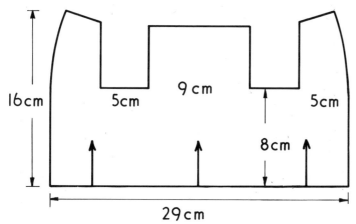

Fig 28   Method of joining up pattern pieces for doll's sun-suit so that only two pieces are worked

JACKET

Make an approx. length of ch to fit the lower edge. Work 6 rows in white, then continue in colour. At armhole level, divide stitches, using a ruler to measure. Work across the two fronts, decreasing at front edges to shape the curve. At shoulder level, shape shoulder in the usual way, adding an extra half row at neck edge. Leave space for armhole as pattern, and work across back finishing in a straight line. Sew shoulder seams. Finish with 2 rows of dc in white, round armholes and fronts, working on the right side for the first row, on the wrong side for the second. Embroider a white lazy-daisy flower on the fronts.

PANTS

Start in white with a length of chain to fit pattern. Make 4 rows dc. Change to colour, and continue, adjusting crochet to the shape of pattern. Finish with 4 rows in white. Sew side seams. Work 1 row of 1 dc 1 ch round top. Slot it with either a fine elastic or a chain to tie at the front. (This outfit is fetching on a Teddy Bear, too!)

Sun-suit for child

It is an easy step to make a similar outfit for a child. Copy Fig 28, using the child's measurements—length of jacket and chest. Pants pattern is made from an easy waist measurement and depth from waist to crutch, or even copied from a pair in current use.

Or, use a paper pattern which fits and draw your pattern from that. Make it exactly as described for the doll, following pattern for guide. Choose your own stitches and arrangement of colours, e.g. a white jacket with coloured border. This is where originality and imagination come in. 6 ozs yarn will make it for a child of five, and a man-made yarn might be advisable.

The long, long waistcoat

Some readers may remember the days of the hug-me-tight. The name was so commonplace that it evoked not the flicker of a smile and the fashion lasted a long time, as fashions did, fifty years ago. It was a short, sleeveless jacket, warm and body-hugging, and came after the Victorian shawl and before the cardigan. It was crocheted either in plain colours or variegated stripes and was a very popular garment. Now it has returned to fashion in an elongated form, approved by the young, comfortable and smart for anyone.

Here is a chance to work from a paper pattern, making your crochet to fit.

The waistcoat is:

loose-fitting with no side seams, doesn't meet at centre front;
36-in (91·5-cm) bust size, but can be adapted for any other size;
25 in (63·5 cm) long, but may be longer or shorter;
and took 10 oz DK wool (greys and purple in this case) and Nos 7 and 8 (4·50- and 4·00-mm) hooks.

A crochet stitch is suggested, though any open stitch may be used.

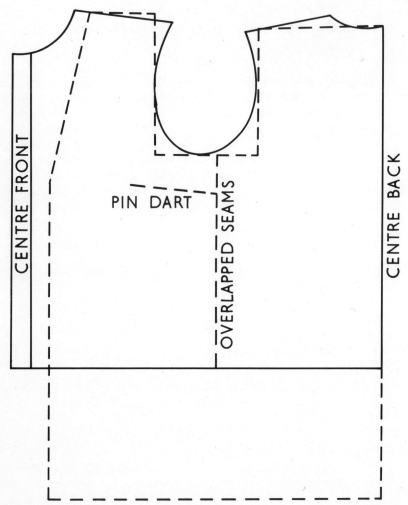

CENTRE FRONT

PIN DART

OVERLAPPED SEAMS

CENTRE BACK

Fig 29   Method of adapting blouse pattern to make a crochet waistcoat

Method

1   Use a plain dress or blouse pattern to fit your size. Cut off turnings.
Eliminate darts by pinning together. Overlap front and back side seams
and pin together. Draw waistcoat pattern on this, following Fig 29.
Trace on to double paper to make complete pattern and cut out.

2 Make a loose chain, a multiple of four, the width of pattern less 2 in (5 cm) to allow for border. (140 sts for 36 in size.)

3 Crochet pattern consists of two rows:

Row 1: 1 tr into 4th ch, tr to end. 3 ch, turn.
Row 2: Miss first st, * 3 tr into front loop only of next st, 1 ch, miss 3 sts, rep from *. After final 3 tr gr, miss 1 ch, 1 tr, 3 ch, turn.

Repeat these two rows, varying the stripes of colour not necessarily evenly, until bust position is reached, after 15 in (38 cm) in my case.

4 *Shape fronts* Starting at front edge on a tr row, dec 1 st at beginning of row. Work to beginning of 5th gr, turn, dec 1 st at front edge of this row. Rep for two more rows, until 1 gr is eliminated. Work 17 rows altogether on the first 4 grs (starting with 3 ch, ending with 1 tr). Work the last two rows in tr. Rep in reverse for left front.

5 Leaving 5 grs unworked for armholes at each side, work across back for 15 rows.

6 Press lightly, join shoulder seams.

7 *Front border* Join on wool at lower right front corner, work 2 dc at edge of every row and 1 dc in each stitch across back of neck, then down left front. Turn, change to No 8 (4·00-mm) hook. Work 7 rows in dc, decreasing at shoulder joins to shape neck.

8 *Sleeve border* Work as for front border, decreasing at each lower corner to round off the shape.

Sleeveless coat

To make a sleeveless, collarless coat, similar to the long waistcoat, 36 in (91·5 cm), length at centre back, you will need 22 oz double knitting wool and No 8 (4·00-mm) hook.

In this case, greater width is needed at the hem and this width should equal the hip measurement. Decreasing at the side seam position will bring the width to bust size. Using a plain dress pattern with shaped side seam, follow instructions on Fig 29. (Adapting blouse pattern for waistcoat.) The pattern will look like Fig 30 (dotted lines).

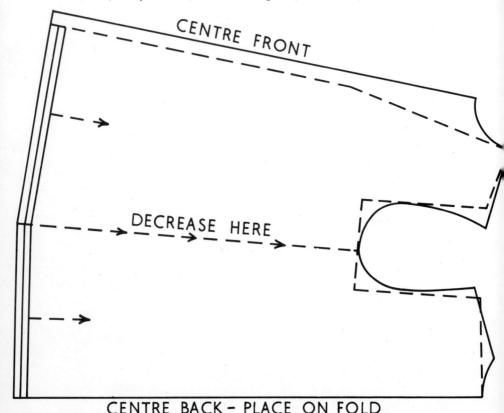

Fig 30   Method of adapting dress pattern for a sleeveless crochet coat

Choose your stitch—a pretty semi-open stitch with borders of double crochet would be suitable—and work as for waistcoat, starting at the hem. After the first 6 rows of pattern, mark side-seam positions with coloured threads and decrease every 6 rows until crochet fits pattern at bust level.

Continue and finish as for waistcoat.

Star-stitch jacket

Plate 41   Jacket in star stitch with ring buttons

The method described has so far been used for sleeveless garments. This
jacket with long sleeves is equally easy to make from a shirt-blouse
pattern. Fig 31 shows alteration of pattern.

The blouse sleeve is shaped with a vent gathered into a cuff. This has
been narrowed at the wrist and now measures $8\frac{1}{2}$ in (21·5 cm).

The shirt-type collar can be copied in crochet, and after it is attached to
the jacket, a border of double crochet is added to the fronts and round
the collar.

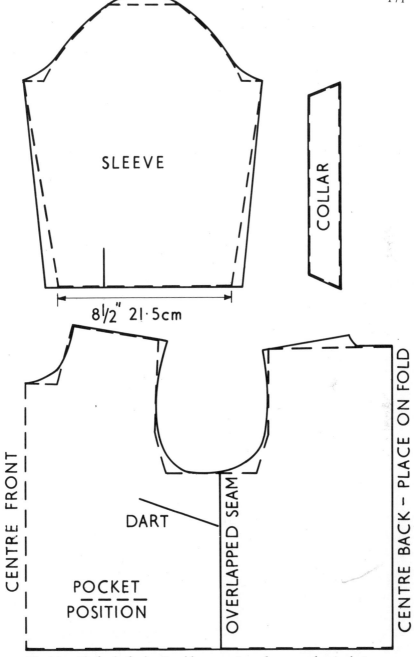

Fig 31   Method of adapting blouse pattern for a crochet jacket

Adapting pattern

1   Pin darts. Cut off seam allowance except side seams. Cut off
allowance at centre front line.

2   Overlap side seam allowance and pin together.

3   Shape armhole curves as in diagram, also sleeve curves. Narrow
sleeve at wrist.

4   Mark pocket position. (Optional) $4\frac{1}{2}$ in (11·5 cm).

5   Lengthen or shorten if necessary.

6   Place pattern on large double sheet of folded paper with centre back
to fold. Trace new shape with tracing wheel or carbon paper then cut
out.

7   You now have a full-sized pattern showing shape to be crocheted.

Method

Approximate numbers of stitches are given for a jacket size 36-in (91·5-
cm) bust. For this you will need 18–20 oz double knitting wool, No 7
(4·50-mm) hook, No 9 (3·50 mm) for border.

Instructions for star stitch, see page 135.

Make 136 ch, add turning ch and work in star st to pocket level. For
pocket, make ch $4\frac{1}{2}$ in (11·5 cm), pass over equivalent number of
stitches, continue in pattern to 2nd pocket, rep, then continue to end of
row. Work on ch sts on return row. Work to armhole level.

RIGHT FRONT

Work across 17 stars for 16 rows to top of rever, then complete
shoulder, decreasing 1 star at neck edge for 3 star rows. In the last row
of stars, shape shoulder by working 7 stars, then dc to armhole edge
(armhole to shoulder = 11 star rows).

LEFT FRONT

Work similarly. Complete pocket flaps (4 star rows).

BACK

Leaving 6 stars unworked at each armhole, work across back for 11 star rows. No shaping on shoulders and neck, leave a straight line. Press lightly and sew shoulder seam.

SLEEVES

36 ch = 18 stars. Work straight for 4 star rows, then increase at each side to fit pattern. At armhole level, leave 3 stars unworked at each side, continue to shape by decreasing at each edge to fit top of sleeve. Top of sleeve is left straight with 6 stars.

Press. Sew sleeve seams. Pin sleeve to armhole on right side, matching lines of star stitch. Ease in top 6 stars to fit top of shoulder. Draw together carefully to make neat join. Make collar, sew on, make border of dc 1 in wide round fronts and collar, with buttonholes on right front. Sew on ring buttons. (See page 39.)

Warm coat with hood

Plate 42   Child's anorak made in double crochet and lined throughout

To fit a four-year-old.

This coat is made entirely in double crochet, lined throughout and
zipped up the front. The hood is attached to the fronts. Instructions are

given by measurements only in the continental manner, so that the crochet pieces are made to fit the pattern. As an exercise in the metric system, all measurements are given in centimetres, though inches are shown in the diagram. By now, you should have a tape measure with centimetres! Larger or smaller sizes can be made by cutting a similar shape from a dressmaking coat pattern, cutting off all turnings (which are not required) and adding a hood.

For this size you will need

12 oz double knitting wool, plain or tweed mixture
1 oz contrast for edges
Nos 7 and 9 (4·50- and 3·50-mm) hooks
18-in (45·5-cm) open zip

Method

First draw the pattern, full size, on firm paper and cut out. Mark all measurements for reference.

RIGHT FRONT

Commence at the hem with a chain measuring 24 cm. (32 ch). Work in dc for 19 cm to pocket level. Work 7 cm from side seam then a ch of 11 cm. Miss an equal number of dc, then continue in dc to end of row. On return row work dc into the 11 ch. Continue to armhole level, decreasing at side seam 3 times to shape seam, until work measures 33 cm, and 21 cm across chest.

Decrease at armhole edge until width across chest is 16 cm. Work straight for 15 cm to shoulder level. Shape shoulder over 5 rows to fit pattern, when work should measure 51 cm and shoulder, 9 cm. Starting at centre front, work across 7 cm, then add a ch measuring 7 cm for the base of hood. Work across these stitches, 14 cm, increasing to make the shape of the hood until it is 18 cm across, then decreasing on each row until work measures 10 cm. Hood will be 24 cm in height. Break off.

Complete pocket flap, working 8 rows dc on the 11 stitches at opening. Add three rows dc in contrast wool, sew ends neatly to finish.

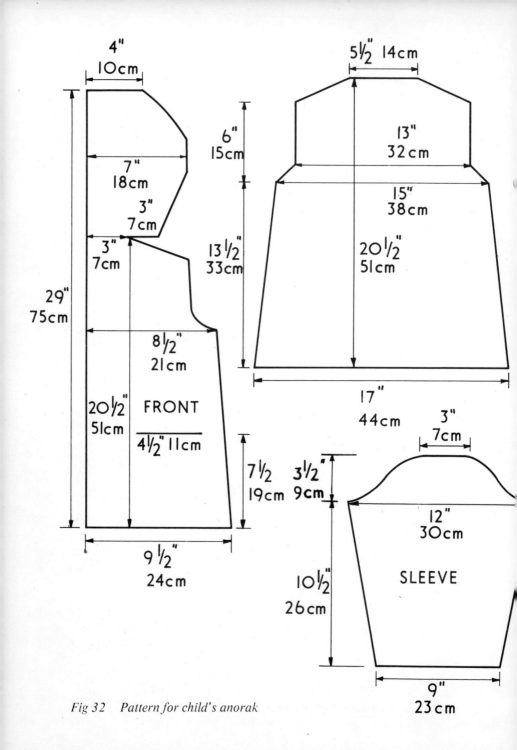

Fig 32   Pattern for child's anorak

LEFT FRONT

Make the same and reverse.

BACK

Commence with a ch of 44 cm (59 ch). Work to armhole level, decreasing at side seams to correspond with fronts and until work measures 33 cm in length and 38 cm in width. Decrease at armhole until width is 32 cm. Then work straight for 15 cm to shoulder level. Shape shoulders as for front over 5 rows bringing full length to 51 cm and neck measuring 14 cm.

SLEEVE

Start at the wrist with a ch measuring 23 cm (31 ch). Increase regularly, following pattern, until work measures 26 cm in length and 30 cm across. Work for another 9 cm, shaping the top to correspond with pattern. Make another, similarly.

PUTTING TOGETHER

Using pattern, cut out a lining in cotton poplin, or choice, allowing turnings of 2 cm. Cut also pocket linings about 13-cm square. Make these into pocket bags and sew to the crochet edges of pockets. Stitch all seams of lining and hood. Press.

Draw the side seams of crochet together, join shoulders and seam the two hood pieces together. Join hood to back of neck. Join sleeve seams and sew in to jacket. Starting at the right front, with No 9 hook, work with contrast wool in dc making an edging on fronts and round hood. Work two more rows. Press fronts. Similarly, work 3 rows dc at cuff edge, and turn back narrow cuff. Lay the zip under the fronts, pin and tack carefully and sew by hand in backstitch through the crochet. Pin in the lining and hem firmly.

Child's skirt

Plate 43   Little girl's skirt which can easily be enlarged widthways and lengthways as the child grows

One of the first signs that a little girl is growing up is the day she displays a vehement desire for a skirt—like her mum! At the age of three or four she's still rather rotund and waistless, which makes for problems. Straps over shoulders can be untidy, so something with a good grip of that non-existent waist is necessary.

I have found this pattern excellent, not only because it grips and stays in place but because as the child grows, so can the skirt, widthways and lengthways, until you and she tire of it.

The pattern given is for a three- to four-year-old. Simple calculations will produce a bigger size; it is hardly likely that you'll need a smaller!

Measurements

Length 9 in (22·5 cm).

Waist 22 in (50 cm).

You will need

3 oz 4-ply wool, dark colour
2 oz 4-ply wool, lighter or contrast
No 8 (4·00-mm) hook
A waist-length piece of 1-in (2·5-cm) binding, and elastic

(Buy an extra ounce of each colour if you think she's going to wear it for ever.)

Method

Working lengthways in panels of dark and light, wool is not broken off, but carried across waist edge for alternate panels.

In dark colour, make 42 ch, plus 1 ch to turn.

Row 1: 9 dc, 33 htr, 2 ch, turn.

Row 2: 33 htr, 9 dc, 1 ch, turn.

Rep these two rows twice, making 6 rows.

Row 7: Join on light wool. 9 dc. 33 htr worked into back loops only of previous row. This gives a pleated effect. 2 ch, turn.

Row 8: As row 2.

Row 9: As row 1.

Row 10: As row 2.

Change to dark wool, always working first row of htrs into back loops, as in row 7.

These 10 rows complete the pattern. Work until the top measures 22 in (50 cm) on required waist size.

Join up seam, sew binding to top, turn back making a casing. Binding should not show above crochet. Insert elastic for extra 'grip'.

TO ENLARGE

Unpick seam, add further panels as necessary.

Rows of htrs in dark colour around hem-line will increase length.

Child's pinafore dress

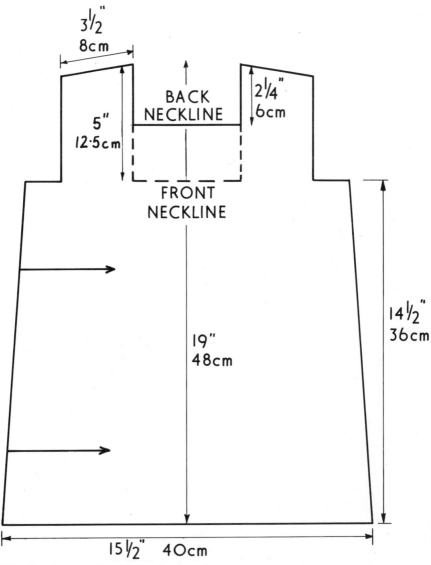

Fig 33   Pattern for child's pinafore dress

Here is an example of a vertically crocheted dress made following a
paper pattern. Although this is made, and instructions are given for a
four-year-old, the method can easily be adapted to any size, working
from a pattern that fits. A coloured front panel gives interest.

You will need

5 oz Paton's Fiona in main colour
Oddments of 3 colours for panel, A, B and C, about $\frac{1}{2}$ oz of each.
No 7 (4·50-mm) hook

Method

BACK

Starting at side seam make 52 ch.

Row 1: 50 htrs. *Turn every row with 2 ch.*

Rows 2 and 3: 29 htr, 1 ss, turn, 1 ss into previous ss, 29 htr.

Row 4: 29 htr, 1 htr into ss, 20 htr.

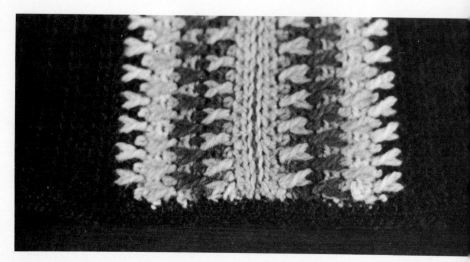

Plate 44   Detail of coloured front panel in pinafore dress

Row 5: 50 htr (shaping at side seam completed).

Work 3 more rows then add 16 ch for shoulder. 66 sts.

Work 9 rows on these sts, increasing 1 st at end of 4th and 6th rows. 68 sts *.

Next row: 60 htr.

Work 13 rows on these 60 sts.

Next row: 60 htr, 8 ch.

Now work 2nd shoulder as first, decreasing 1 st at beginning of 4th and 6th rows for shaping.

Complete back by working in reverse, to side seam.

FRONT

This is made in two pieces, joined in the centre. Follow instructions for back as far as *. Make two. Break off wool.

Panel: Join on colour A at hem edge of right front.

Row 1: 1 htr, 1 long htr alternately for 50 sts. Long htr: woh, insert hook horizontally between 2nd and 3rd sts *2 rows below*, woh, draw through loop, pull loops 1 in long, equal to depth of 2 rows, woh, draw through.

Row 2: Htrs. Break off.

Row 3: Join on colour B. 1 long htr, 1 htr alternately, 50 sts.

Row 4: Htrs. Break off.

Row 5: Join on colour C, rep row 1.

Row 6: As row 2.

Row 7: Join on colour B. Rep rows 3 and 4. Break off.

On left front work panel similarly but starting from the 18th st from shoulder, working down to the hem.

Make a neat join down centre front and press lightly.

Join shoulder seams. Work 2 rows dc round neck. Press.

Join side seams and press. Work 2 rows dc round armholes.

Rows of dc may be worked around hem in main colour and, of course, more rows may be added to increase length when needed.

All-in-one first garment for a baby

A small baby should be dressed with as few garments and as little fuss as possible. Its clothes should be easily washable and dry-able, non-shrinkable and needing no ironing. One's usual view of a young baby is its top half which should be pretty. Its bottom half is the business of its mother and should be easy to manipulate.

Plate 45   All-in-one first garment for a baby

This top-cum-pilch fulfils all these requirements: is made from 3-ply bri-nylon or similar yarn in an open stitch which is warm like a string vest. Its shape is geometrical as the diagram shows. Quite easy, therefore, to enlarge the pattern for a bigger baby of six or nine months when the practicability still holds.

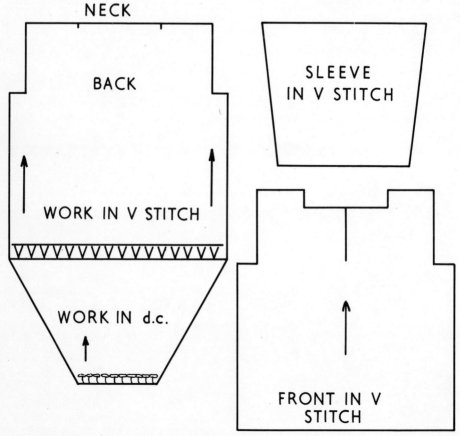

Fig 34   Pattern for all-in-one first garment for a baby

You will need

3 oz 3-ply bri-nylon
Nos 9 and 12 (3·50- and 2·50-mm) hooks
3 small buttons for front opening
4 large buttons for pilch opening

Method

BACK

Make 18 ch plus 1 turning ch. Work 8 rows of 18 dc.

Continuing in dc, inc 1 st at *each* end of *each* row until you have 58 sts. (50 rows from beginning.) 2 ch, turn.

Next row: * Miss 1 sp, 2 tr in next sp, * rep to end, finish with 1 tr, 2 ch, turn.

Next and following 25 rows: * Miss 1 sp, 2 tr in first tr of 'v' stitch *. Rep from * to end, finish with 1 tr, 2 ch, turn. (28 'v' sts.)

27th row: *Armhole*   Ss over 5 sts, 2 ch, 'v' st to last 6 sts, 1 tr, 2 ch, turn. (24 'v' sts.)

Work 10 rows on these sts, fasten off, leaving end for sewing.

FRONT

Make 58 ch and 1 turning ch. Work 1 row dc, 2 ch, turn.

Work in 'v' st to correspond with back, making 26 rows.

27th row: Ss over 5 sts, then work to centre front. Turn and work 8 rows on these sts, starting and finishing row with 1 tr.

Next row: 7 'v' sts.

Work 2 more rows on these sts. Fasten off.

Work left front to correspond.

Sew shoulder seams, 16 sts across back at each end.

SLEEVE

Make 2 tr in each sp across armhole. (44 tr, 22 'v' sts.) Continue across these sts, decreasing 1 st at each end until 18 'v' sts remain.

Work until 16 rows are completed.

Rep on 2nd armhole.

Press lightly.

MAKING UP

Join side seams. Sew first two rows of sleeve to base of armhole, then join remainder of sleeve seam.

Using No 12 hook, work 1 row dc at wrist. Finish with edging as follows:

3 dc, 3 ch, 1 ss into same stitch as last dc. Repeat.

Finish base of garment similarly, round pilch and across front, but using No 9 hook.

NECK FINISH

With No 12 (2·50 mm) hook start at neck edge and work 4 rows dc down under-lap side, then 1 row dc round neck and down upper side of opening.

Turn and work three buttonholes in next row: * 3 dc, 2 ch, miss 2 ch, rep from * twice. Turn, work 1 row dc down front. Turn, and work edging as before up front opening and around neck.

Sew across centre front opening. Sew on buttons at centre, and at pilch opening after strengthening with a strip of ribbon.

'V' stitches serve as buttonholes for pilch and may be reinforced with oversewing.

Epilogue

Though it is usual to preface a book of this kind with a history of the craft, the origins of crochet are so lost in obscurity that it seemed wiser to have none. Obviously crochet is a very ancient craft, probably older than knitting, the manipulation of a single tool being simpler than the complicated use of two.

We know that knitting was found on corpses preserved in peat from the Teutonic Bronze Age—third to first centuries B.C., so we can assume that crochet was in vogue before that. We know too that the Egyptian garment, the kalasiris, worn in 1000 B.C. was sometimes of a clinging, knitted material which might also have been crochet. Some authorities claim that the ancient Greeks plied their hooks, which they might well have done in view of their achievements in other more intellectual spheres. None of this, it seems to me, matters very much. What does matter is that crochet was very nearly forgotten during the last forty years and that a craft so easy and pleasant to do should not be allowed to disappear. We have the sad example of lace-making in this country; many of the old patterns and methods have been lost because they were not passed on to younger generations.

So if you have a daughter, a granddaughter, a niece or great-niece, teach her to crochet now. Even if the present, possibly ephemeral, fashion passes, she will have absorbed the technique. The young retain their learning and may be grateful some day for your tuition and patience. You run only to boys in your family? Some are receptive and like using their hands, so why not teach them too?